French Philosophers

and

New-England Transcendentalism

BY

WALTER L. LEIGHTON

GREENWOOD PRESS, PUBLISHERS
NEW YORK   1968

LIBRARY OF CONGRESS catalogue card number: 68-19289

Printed in the United States of America

To

C. W. K.

WHO HAS GIVEN ME BOTH THE ENCOURAGEMENT

AND OPPORTUNITY FOR THE WRITING

OF THIS THESIS

PREFACE

THE writings of the Transcendentalists of New England have been from youth of especial interest to me. An investigation of the phenomena of New-England Transcendentalism was instigated by a reading of the chapter on Transcendentalism in Professor Barrett Wendell's *Literary History of America*. The idea of making a specialty of the French influence in its relation to New-England Transcendentalism as a subject for a doctorate thesis was intimated to me by Professor LeB. R. Briggs, Dean of the Harvard University faculty.

Thanks for assistance in the course of actually drawing up the dissertation are due — first, to Dr. Albert Lefevre, professor of philosophy at the University of Virginia, for valuable suggestions concerning the definition of Transcendentalism; next, to Dr. R. H. Wilson and adjunct-professor Dr. E. P. Dargan, of the department of Romance Languages at the University of Virginia, for kind help in the work of revision and correction, and, finally, to Dr. Charles W. Kent, professor at the head of the department of English at the University of Virginia, for general supervision of my work on the thesis.

In the work of compiling and writing the thesis I have been swayed by two motives: first, the purpose to gather by careful research and investigation certain definite facts concerning the French philosophers and the Transcendental movement in New England; and, secondly, the desire to set forth the information amassed in a cursory and readable style.

W. L. L.

April 15, 1908.

CONTENTS

I

INTRODUCTION

II

FRENCH EXPOSITORS OF TRANSCENDENTALISM

III

RELATION OF NEW-ENGLAND TRANSCENDENTALISTS TO FRENCH PHILOSOPHERS

IV

CONCLUSION

French Philosophers and New-England Transcendentalism

I. INTRODUCTION

1. DEFINITION OF TRANSCENDENTALISM

IT has been said that when an Englishman has a particular matter to investigate he ventures first to the place of his subject; makes researches and takes notes there for two years; and then, returning to England, draws up a cursory account of it all in two weeks. The Frenchman journeys to the vicinity of his subject; pursues researches there for about two weeks; and then, returning to France, spends two years in writing up a gracious essay. And the German, when he has a matter for investigation, retires forthwith into his sanctum, isolates himself there for days and days, and gradually evolves in the course of time out of his inner consciousness a prolix dissertation.

However trifling this intimation may be in view of such scientific investigations as have been carried on in England by Charles Darwin, in France by Ernest Renan regarding the Bible, and in Germany by Friedrich Wolf concerning the Homeric question, — the fact remains that Kant, the German metaphysician, has succeeded in framing one of the most abstract and at the same time most lucid and final definitions as yet made of Transcendentalism, and has framed it, too, as it were, largely out of his inner consciousness.

The acutely rational *Transcendentalphilosophie* of Kant deals with the sources and scope of knowledge.[1] He would have us understand by transcendental knowledge, theoretical knowledge about the necessary principles of all knowledge. Our knowledge about the world of experience, he tells us — in defining transcen-

[1] Cf. Immanuel Kant, sein Leben und seine Lehre, Frommann's Klassiker der Philosophy.

dental knowledge — is necessarily founded upon *a priori* principles. *A priori*, for Kant, is knowledge in advance of all experience, that is, knowledge of the content of any of the concepts or principles of thought; and the necessary principles of attaining knowledge are themselves *a priori*, transcendent of experience.

Kant, the critic of pure reason, however, carefully discriminates between *transcendent* and *Transcendental*. The term transcendent applies to whatever lies beyond the realm of knowledge and experience. The extension of concepts, valid within experience, to what is beyond experience — for instance, with reference to God — is a transcendent use of concepts; this transcendent use is, according to Kant and later precise philosophers, illegitimate, and has a bad sense. The term *Transcendental*, on the contrary, has in the philosophy of punctilious Kant a good sense: it is explicitly applied to the *a priori* and necessary factors in experience, not extending beyond experience but only beyond empirically given facts of experience. The term *transcendent* in the bad sense — after the manner of the Scholasticism of the Middle Ages — is opposed, moreover, to the modern principle of divine immanency.[1] But Kant distinctly refutes this transcendent in the sense of the Scholasticism of the Middle Ages, and would have his Transcendental principles construed in an immanent sense, that is as remaining within the limits of experience. Pantheism, which incarnates the immanency theory, is akin in certain respects to the Transcendentalism of Kant; both philosophies hold to the presence of God in the universe.

There are, to be sure, in the history of philosophy, a variety of conceptions of Transcendentalism. The definitions are not especially important, but they help us nevertheless in a way to get down to the matter at hand. Aristotle (384–322 B. C.) held for instance as Transcendental that which in the "transcendent" sense extended beyond the bounds of human experience. F. W. von Schelling (1775–1854) comprehended as Transcendental, in the modern meaning of the word, that which explains matter and all that is objective as the product of mind.[2] Coleridge (1772–1834) tells us in his imaginative literary way that the German

---

[1] Cf. The philosophy of Hegel.
[2] Cf. The philosophy of Bishop Berkeley.

Mystics and Transcendentalists — particularly Bëhmen and Schelling — "contributed to keep alive the heart in the head; gave me an indistinct, yet stirring and working presentiment, that all the products of the mere reflective faculty partook of death, and were as the rattling twigs and sprays in winter, into which a sap was yet to be propelled, from some root to which I had not penetrated, if they were to afford my soul either food or shelter." Ralph Waldo Emerson (1803–1882) states in a distinctly nineteenth century vein that " mankind have ever been divided into two sects, Materialists and Idealists; the first class founding on experience, the second on consciousness. . . . Whatever belongs to the class of intuitive thought is properly called at the present day Transcendental." And W. H. Channing, of our own time, writes after the manner of Emerson, — " Amidst materialists, zealots, and skeptics, the Transcendentalist believed in perpetual inspiration, the miraculous power of will, and a birthright to universal good. He sought to hold communion face to face with the unnameable spirit of his spirit, and gave himself up to the embrace of nature's beautiful joy, as a babe seeks the breast of a mother."

Modern philosophers and men of letters — such as Schelling, Coleridge, and the New-England Transcendentalists — have been, it is clear, whether consciously so or not, decidedly instrumental in blurring and abolishing the acute Kantian distinction of the latter eighteenth century between " transcendent " and Transcendentalism. As a consequence, Transcendentalism — or Nativism — is at the present time widely in vogue in a loose sense as the generic term for various theories which advocate that this or that is *a priori*, — native, inherent, constitutional; it is employed to designate the philosophy of such men of letters as Wordsworth, the philosophy of innate ideas and intuition. Empiricism, on the other hand, may be regarded at present as the generic term widely in vogue for divers theories which attribute the origin of all our knowledge to experience *a posteriori;* it is employed to designate the philosophy of such modern scientists as Ernst Haeckel, the philosophy of sensationalism and materialism.

To understand better the philosophy of Transcendentalism, let us examine briefly the philosophy of Empiricism — the other extreme of philosophic thought as opposed to Transcendentalism.

To the doctrine which admits of nothing as true except what is the result of experience, rejecting all *a priori* knowledge, the term Empiricism is applied. René Descartes (1596–1650) gives us in the following resolutions, which he drew up for himself as a kind of philosophical code, the viewpoint of the Empiricist: " Le premier — de ne recevoir jamais aucune chose pour vraie que je ne la connusse évidemment être telle; c'est-à-dire d'éviter soigneusement la précipitation et la prévention, et de ne comprendre rien de plus en mes jugements que ce qui se présenterait si clairement et si distinctement à mon esprit, que je n'eusse aucune occasion de le mettre en doute. Le second, de diviser chacune des difficultés que j'examinerais en autant de parcelles qu'il se pourrait et qu'il serait requis pour les mieux résoudre. Le troisième, de conduire par ordre mes pensées en commençant par les objets les plus simples, et les plus aisés à connaître, pour monter peu à peu comme par degrés jusques à la connaissance des plus composés, et supposant même de l'ordre entre ceux qui ne se précèdent point naturellement les uns les autres. Et le dernier, de faire partout des dénombrements si entiers et des revues si générales, que je fusse assuré de ne rien omettre." [1]

Francis Bacon (1561–1626) was the first in England to formulate the doctrine of Empiricism; he argued that knowledge is the fruit of experience; regarded himself simply as the servant and interpreter of nature; and was the creator of practical and scientific induction. But John Locke (1632–1704) is, one may say, the most flat-footed of all the exponents of Empiricism. He tells us, — " All ideas come from sensation or reflection. Let us then suppose the mind to be white paper void of all characters, without any ideas, how comes it to be furnished? Whence comes it by that vast store which the busy and boundless fancy of man has painted on it, with an almost endless variety. Whence has it all the materials of reason and knowledge? To this I answer, in one word, from experience; in that all our knowledge is founded, and from that it ultimately derives itself."

Failure to understand from the beginning the difference between Empiricism and Transcendentalism may breed confusion. A brief comparison of the two kinds of philosophy may then, as a final word, be illuminating.

[1] Discours de la méthode, 1637. René Descartes.

Transcendentalism, at the present time, in a general sense, is the doctrine that man has a knowledge of philosophic principles by an immediate beholding without the process of reason or aid of experience. Empiricism, on the other hand, is in general the doctrine that all knowledge is derived through the senses from experiences. Empiricism tends to subordinate man to nature and experience for all his knowledge of life and eternity; Transcendentalism is disposed to subordinate nature and experience to man. Empiricism is objective; Transcendentalism is subjective. Transcendentalism depending over-much upon intuition tends to become vague, visionary, fantastic; and Empiricism depending over-much upon sensation and experience tends to become materialistic, matter-of-fact, mechanical. One might say that the ambiguous and extravagant utterances of so-called clairvoyants represent absurd phases of Transcendentalism; and that the crude experiments and glittering generalities of pseudo-scientists denote absurd stages of Empiricism.

2. Miscellaneous Precursors

We believe to-day that all things are the result of evolution or transition; and in the light of this thought we are warranted in holding that the phenomena of New-England Transcendentalism are a result, no less than other things, of natural processes of change and development.

In taking up the subject of the precursors of New-England Transcendentalism, however, we have to do with a complicated matter. It is, in truth, almost impossible to determine definite analogies, and to point to them explicitly as the precursors or sources of the Transcendentalists in New England. Almost all the writings of all times and countries have in all probability percolated into English through translations, and have been more or less influential directly or indirectly on the writings of the New-England Transcendentalists.

Certain preceding writers and writings, nevertheless, must have influenced more than others the votaries of New-England idealism whom we have under consideration. The New-England Transcendentalists themselves mention certain philosophers and poets as sources to which they are indebted for ideas and inspiration; certain critics, too, have discovered authors whom they aver to be in part antecedents of the movement; and, finally, from our own cursory acquaintance with world literature we may detect somewhat distinct analogies between what the New-England Transcendentalists have thought and written and what has been thought and uttered by precursors with similar proclivities.

In an early number of *The Dial*, Emerson asks how the age can be a bad one which gives him, among others, Plato, Plutarch, Saint Augustine, Donne, Sir Thomas Browne. In his essay on "Poetry and Imagination" we come across this sentence: " Socrates, the Indian teachers of the Maia, the Bibles of the nations, Shakespeare, Milton, Hafiz, Ossian, the Welsh Bards,—these all deal with nature and history as means and symbols, and not as ends." And Emerson's friend and literary adviser, Mr. Cabot, sets forth the following factors among others as having been influential on the mind and character of his comrade: Plutarch, Saint Simon, Boederer, Bishop Berkeley, Coleridge, Goethe, Swedenborg, J. Böhme, Neo-Platonists, Hindu philosophy, — Bhagavat Gita, Upanishads, Puramas, Vedas, The Chaldean oracles, Hafiz, Enweri, S. Reid, Fichte, Hegel, Schleiermacher, and Greek Mythology.[1]

Passing to Margaret Fuller, we find that in a letter dated June 3, 1833, she writes: " I part with Plato with regret. . . . Eutyphon is excellent. 'T is the best specimen I have ever seen of that mode of convincing. . . . Crito I have read only once but like it. . . . The Apology I deem only remarkable for the noble tone of sentiment, and beautiful calmness." Mr. Frothingham, too, in his book on New-England Transcendentalism,[2] gives the following authors as among those who appealed to Margaret Fuller: Goethe, Novalis, Jean Paul Richter, Wordsworth, Coleridge, Carlyle, Michael Angelo, Dr. Wilkinson the Swedenborgian, Fourier, Rousseau. In his volume, "Concord and Merrimac Rivers," Thoreau quotes among others from such varied authors as Hindu sages, George Herbert, and Milton. And, finally, a certain Mr. Johnson, in an

---

[1] Memoir of Ralph Waldo Emerson, James Elliott Cabot, 2 vols., H., M. & Co., Cambridge, 1887.

[2] Transcendentalism in New England, O. B. Frothingham, Am. Unit. Assoc., Boston, 1903.

article entitled "Transcendentalism,"[1] writes of the authors in general who helped to promote the movement: "From Descartes and Spinoza it descended through Leibnitz and Kant, and their later interpreters, Cousin and Jouffroy. It was developed in various forms by Schelling, Hegel, and the higher German metaphysics, and formed an essential part of the English and Scotch philosophies of Cudworth, Reid, and Hamilton, of the idealism of Coleridge and of the moral intensity of Carlyle."

Out of these specific references, and other general data, we can abstract at least six influences on the New England Transcendentalists which preponderate over the rest; these six sources of influence are of Hindu, Persian, Greek, German, English, and French origin.

The fame of the literature and philosophy of the Hindu-Aryan people is not widespread. But scholars like Monier Williams and Max Müller have determined upon and brought to light much interesting matter. The following is a suggestive list of the notable productions of the Hindus: the "Hymns of the Veda," the "Upanishad" and "Bhagavadgéta" writings, the "Law Books of Menu," and the "Hetopadésa" (or Book of Good Council).

These writings of the Hindus tend, broadly speaking, to fix our attention on the Infinite and Eternal, on the regions which lie beyond human ken, on the whence and the wherefore of all things. They stand for the subjugation of the senses, for a life of reason and moderation, and uphold as blissful a kind of super-conscious state, an at-one-ness in freedom and tranquillity with the Life of the Universe that ever has been and ever will be. Transcendentalism, indeed, seems to have first manifested itself in pronounced yet quite mild form among the Hindus.

In the "Kartha Upanishad" we find a passage quite characteristic of Hindu occultism, — " If the slayer thinks I slay, if the slain thinks I am slain, then both of them do not know well; it (the Soul) does not slay nor is it slain."[2] The lines bear a striking resemblance to a stanza, which seems almost a paraphrase of the passage in the "Kartha Upanishad," — in one of Emerson's poems entitled "Brahma," —

---

[1] Transcendentalism, S. Johnson, *Radical Review*, Boston, Jan. 1, 1884.
[2] *Bibliotheca India*, Calcutta, 1852.

> "If the red slayer thinks he slays,
> Or if the slain think he is slain,
> They know not well the subtle ways
> I keep, and pass, and turn again." [1]

From the Persians, a numerous and important branch of the
Iranian group of the Aryan stock, have sprung not a few of the
world's scholars, philosophers, and poets, But of all kinds of
literary expression, the country is most noteworthy for its Oriental
poetry. And the chief figures of the Persian Parnassus according
to one of our New-England Transcendentalists, are: Firdausi,
Enweri, Nisami, Jelaleddin, Saadi, Hafiz, and Jami.

One of the poems of Enweri, mystically symbolical of body and
soul, has been rendered into English verse by Emerson:

> " A painter in China once painted a hall;
> Such a web never hung on an emperor's wall;
> One half from his brush with rich colors did run,
> The other he touched with a beam of the sun;
> So that all which delighted the eye in one side,
> The same, point for point, in the other replied.
> In thee, friend, that Tyrian chamber is found;
> Thine the star-pointing-roof, and the base on the ground;
> Is one half depicted with colors less bright?
> Beware that the counterpart blazes with life!" [2]

The most celebrated philosophers of Greece were Hellenes, a
branch of the same Indo-European race as the Hindus and Persians. They may be divided into two classes, — (1) the philosophers of nature, such as Heraclitus and Democritus; and (2) the
philosophers of nature and man, such as Socrates, Plato, and
Aristotle. These philosophers, together with the Greek dramatists,
were doubtless, in some measure, influential in their utterance on
the Transcendentalists of New England. We make selections
from the writings of one or two with a view to intimating their
penchant toward Transcendentalism.

Heraclitus (535–475 B. C.), known among the ancients as the

[1] Poems, H., M. & Co., p. 170.
[2] Body and Soul, Enweri, from Emerson's Persian Poetry.

obscure, or the weeping philosopher, but withal, broad of outlook, deep of insight, sane, writes: " There is properly no existence but only becoming, that is, a continual passing from one existence into another." In a similar strain Emerson says: " Power ceases the instant of repose; it resides in the moment of transition from a past to a present state, in the shooting of the gulf, in the darting to an aim." [1]

Plato (427-347 B. C.), a man of letters as well as idealistic philosopher of high order, the disciple of Socrates and the teacher of Aristotle, declares: " Through Love all the intercourses and converse of God with man, whether awake or asleep, is carried on. The wisdom which understands this is spiritual; all other wisdom, such as that of arts and handicrafts, is mean and vulgar." [2] We have to compare with this an analogous passage from Sylvester Judd, a New-England clergyman and novelist of idealistic tendencies, who lived and wrote during the flood-tide of Transcendentalism in New England:

"Love is my food, my bed,
And roof. Love is my wing, my impulsive love,
And soul and circumstances, my joy and prayer.
In love I dwell in God, and God in me.
Not otherwise is seen the great Unseen." [3]

The dramatist Euripides, who embodies the spirit of his age, and depicts human nature as it is, appears now and then in a passage to be a bit Transcendental: from Hippolytus, —

"Try first thyself, and after call on God;
For to the worker God himself lends aid."

With this compare again certain lines from Emerson, —

"Trust thyself: every heart vibrates to that iron string."

The character and genius of the Greeks have, in fact, exercised powerful influence on the life and thought of the civilized world. Out of crude beginnings they developed wonderful harmony of

[1] Self-Reliance, Essays, First Series, p. 45 ff., H., M. & Co., Cambridge, 1895.
[2] Symposium — Source Book of Greek Philosophy, C. M. Bakewell.
[3] Philo — An Evangeliad, 1850.

body and mind. Belief in themselves, love of glory, freedom of religion, philosophical impulses, — all helped to mould their character and determine the quality of their utterance. Their drama and philosophy, as well as their arts, are distinguished by depth, intellectual completeness, philosophical vividness. Without the Greek influence a deal that is Transcendental would never have come into being.

Of all people, however, Oriental or Occidental, the Germans plunge deepest and soar highest in the realm of Transcendentalism. Their poets and philosophers look far back into the past and peer far forward into the future. They are subjective like the Hindus, rather than objective, as were in large measure the Greeks. But their subjectivity is creative, assertive, renascent. They become now and then, as it were, intoxicated by the vastness of their own conceptions, sublimated by the depth and vitality of their own imaginings.

Kant (1724–1804), the critic of pure reason, would rivet our attention on two august facts:

"The starry heavens above,
And the moral law within."

And both the sense and spirit of this couplet were familiar to the New-England Transcendentalists. James Freeman Clarke, one of the members of the Transcendentalist Club, in characterizing his intimate friend, Theodore Parker, the noteworthy Unitarian preacher, writes in a similar strain: " He (Parker) belonged to that school of thinkers who are called Transcendentalists; who believe that man, as God's child, receives an inheritance of ideas from within; that he knows by insight; that he has intuitions of truth, which furnish the highest evidence of the reality of the soul of God, of Duty, of Immortality." [1] Hegel (1770–1831), after the manner of Heraclitus, declares that God is a process of becoming.[2] And Fichte (1762–1814), by a superb convolution of his cranium, transfers the centre of the universe from wherever else to his own bosom: " This earth of ours with all its splendors which in your

[1] Memoirs, James Freeman Clarke.
[2] History as a Manifestation of Spirit, F. H. Hedge, translation from Hegel.

childish ignorance you fancied yourselves to be in need of; this sun of ours and the thousand times thousand suns which surround it; all the earths which you divine about every one of these thousand times thousand suns: — this whole vast universe, the thought of which makes your soul tremble, is nothing but a faint reflexion of your own endless and forever progressing existence." And certain lines in one of Emerson's essays have, we believe, a somewhat similar ring: " Every true man is a cause, a country, and an age; requires infinite spaces and numbers to accomplish his design." [1]

Transcendentalism, in short, would not be what it is, by a wide margin, were it not for the Germans with their profound learning, subjective intensity, pantheistic spirituality. They are, for the most part, born optimists and idealists. They combine in themselves, and raise to a high degree, the Transcendentalism of Hindu and Greek philosophy.

In regard to the English, it is difficult to determine what to say. They constitute a kind of cross, in the realms of Transcendental philosophy, between the Greeks, Germans, and French — possessing certain merits here and lacking others there, and interfusing throughout all a poetical and philosophical vitality and exuberance all their own. The Elizabethan Age, the Puritan Age, and the Period of Romantic Revival constitute three important epochs in English Literature. And it is during two of these three eras that elements of Transcendentalism, in one form or another, seem now and then definitely to crop out.

A passage from Milton's " Paradise Lost " is noteworthy for grasp of imagination and spiritual insight:

> "One Almighty is, from whom
> All things proceed, and up to Him return,
> If not depraved from good, created all
> Such to perfection; one first matter all,
> Indued with various forms, various degrees
> Of substance, and, in things that live, of life;
> But more refined, more spiritual and pure,
>
> As nearer to him placed or nearer tending
> Each in their several active spheres assigned,

[1] Essays, First Series, H., M. & Co., 1895, p. 61.

> Till body up to spirit work, in bounds
> Proportion'd to each kind. So from the root
> Springs lighter the green stalk, from thence the leaves
> More aery, last the bright consummate flower
> Spirits odorous breathes; flowers and their fruit,
> Man's nourishment, by gradual scale sublim'd,
> To intellectual."

It is interesting to compare with this two passages from the writings of New-England Transcendentalists. The first is from W. E. Channing, — "The voice of our whole nature, properly interpreted, is a cry after a higher existence." [1] And the other is from Emerson, —

> "The subtle chain of countless rings
> The next unto the farthest brings;
> The eye reads omens where it goes,
> And speaks all languages the rose;
> And striving to be man, the worm
> Mounts through the spires of form." [2]

Wordsworth, though, is doubtless the most truly Transcendental of any figure in English Literature. His scope of thought at its best is cosmic; he has faith in an inner light; he is sensitive to the presence and manifestation in all things of the Infinite and Eternal. We quote a characteristic passage from "Tintern Abbey," —

> "A sense sublime
> Of something far more deeply interfused,
> Whose dwelling is the light of setting suns,
> And the round ocean and the living air
> And the blue sky, and the mind of man, —
> A motion and a spirit, that impels
> All thinking things, all objects of all thought,
> And rolls through all things."

And we have to compare with these lines a passage, somewhat analogous, from the writings of Thoreau, the friend and contemporary of Emerson, and one of the most noteworthy of the lesser New-England idealists, — "Sometimes, in a Summer morning,

---

[1] Sermon, William Ellery Channing.
[2] Poems.

having taken my accustomed bath, I sat in my sunny doorway from sunrise till noon, rapt in revery, amidst the pines and hickories and sumachs, in undisturbed solitude and stillness. . . . I grew in these seasons like corn in the night, . . . I realized what the Orientals meant by contemplation and the forsaking of words. . . . If the birds and flowers had tried me by their standard, I should not have been found wanting." [1]

If elements of Transcendentalism are faint in Persian, Greek, and English, they are — from one point of view — fainter still in French literature. The race which produced Molière, Racine, Balzac, and Hugo has, to be sure, an order of genius of first water. But few will dispute that it is not easy to put one's finger upon what is Transcendental in it. The conditions which evolved such blasé rationalists as La Rochefoucauld or Voltaire would hardly allow Transcendental views — after the order of Plato or Kant, Carlyle or Emerson — to be taken too seriously.

But certain figures in French literature appear to manifest in some measure affinity for Transcendentalism. Mr. Frothingham and George Ripley in their volumes [2] appertaining to our subject enable us to compile the following list of French writers as having been more or less interested in the Transcendental in the course of their utterance: Cousin, Jouffroy, Fourier, Paul Janet on Plato, Saint Simon, Barthélemy Saint-Hilaire on Aristotle and Indian Philosophy, Bouillet on Plotinus, Émile Saisset on Spinoza, Tissot and Barni on Kant, J. Simon and E. Vacherot on the Alexandrine School, Cabanis, Laromiguière the successor of Cabanis, and Maine de Biran, who regards *Will* as the base of personality.

The above heterogeneous catalogue as indicative of those in France, related to Transcendentalism in general or to New England Transcendentalism in particular, is for us, indeed, too inclusive. In our opinion — after a careful survey — the writers of France who were prime leaders of the Transcendental movement there and who have really exerted appreciable influence upon and manifested more or less distinct analogy to phases of New-England Transcendentalism, may properly be reduced to three, namely, —

---

[1] Walden, by H. D. Thoreau, H., M. & Co., Cambridge.
[2] (a) Transcendentalism in New England, by O. B. Frothingham;
    (b) Specimens of Foreign Standard Literature, by G. Ripley.

Cousin, Jouffroy, and, in a way, the French Socialist Fourier. And yet it is with this French influence on New-England Transcendentalism, faint and slight as it is, that we are later in this dissertation to be especially concerned.

3. Beginnings in New England

About 1835, Amos Bronson Alcott, the Connecticut Pestalozzi, had achieved as an idealist and an educator quite wide renown. He was an earnest student of Plato and the Bible and a devoted admirer of Carlyle. A band of young men, among whom was F. H. Hedge, urged Alcott at this time to settle permanently in New England and assist them in editing a new magazine which was to be called *The Transcendentalist*.[1] Those most active along with F. H. Hedge in the enterprise were Dr. Channing, Miss Peabody, James Freeman Clarke, and George Ripley. The movement proved to be premature. But out of it grew the publication of *The Dial* and the name Transcendentalists.

In his graceful and forcible history of New-England Transcendentalism, which we have mentioned before, Mr. Frothingham sketches for us what he deems to be the beginning of Transcendentalism in New England. He tells us, — " The circumstances which led to the formation of what was afterwards to be known as the Transcendental Club were these. After the public exercises of the Harvard University Centennial,[2] Sept. 8, 1836, it chanced that R. W. Emerson, George Ripley, F. H. Hedge, and George Putnam met in conversation on the unsatisfactory condition of Unitarian theology, and passed the afternoon in conference in a room at " Willard's." The meeting was adjourned to meet at Mr. Ripley's in Boston the following week; and thence again, in the course of the same month, to Mr. Emerson's in Concord. On this occasion there was a much larger gathering, in cluding A. B. Alcott, C. A. Bartol, G. P. Bradford, C. A. Bronson, W. H. Channing, J. F. Clarke, J. S. Dwight, Convers Francis, Caleb Stetson, Margaret Fuller, and Miss E. P. Peabody. The

---

[1] *Q. v.* Alcott's Diary, March, 1835.
[2] *Q. v.* Emerson's Divinity School Address.

club thus formed, without rules or organization, continued to meet at irregular intervals, according to personal convenience. . . ."

Emerson, with his customary clear vision and sage modesty, gives us half humorously and half seriously in a few lines in his essay entitled " Life and Letters in New England " his version of the incipient stages of the Transcendental movement in New England: " Dr. Channing,[1] whilst he lived, was the star of the American Church, and we then thought, if we do not still think, that he left no successor in the pulpit. He could never be reported, for his eye and voice could not be printed, and his discourses lose their best in losing them. . . . Dr. Channing took counsel in 1840 with George Ripley, to the point whether it were possible to bring cultivated thoughtful people together and make society that deserved the name. He had earlier talked with Dr. John Collins Warren on the like purpose, who had admitted the wisdom of the design and undertook to aid him in making the experiment. Dr. Channing repaired to Dr. Warren's house on the appointed evening, with large thoughts which he wished to open. He found a well-chosen assembly of gentlemen variously distinguished; there was mutual greeting and introduction, and they were chatting agreeably on different matters and drawing gently towards their great expectation, when a side-door opened, the whole company streamed in to an oyster supper, crowned by excellent wines; and so ended the first attempt to establish æsthetic society in Boston."

The term Transcendentalism, then, it may be inferred, grew out of the proposed establishment of a magazine which was to be called *The Transcendentalist*. It may be readily seen, too, that the Unitarian Movement was contemporaneous with the Transcendental Movement in New England; it is probable, indeed, that Unitarianism in New England helped in no small measure to bring Transcendentalism into bloom. There were three periods of Unitarianism: the first, 1815, led by Dr. W. E. Channing; the second, 1836, led by Theodore Parker; the third, 1860, led by Dr. T. H. Hedge. And these three, Channing, Parker, Hedge, were widely known as Transcendentalists as well as Unitarians. The year 1836, however, may be taken as the birth of the

[1] William Ellery Channing (1780-1842), Unitarian Clergyman. He became pastor of the Federal St. Church, Boston, in 1803.

idealistic movement in New England under the name of Transcendentalism, with R. W. Emerson the leader of Transcendentalism, Theodore Parker the leader of Unitarianism, and both
disciples of Dr. W. E. Channing, the chief exponent of the Liberal
Movement in New England of the early nineteenth century.

There was at the time of the beginnings of Transcendentalism
in New England no definite system of philosophy or kind of organization. The prime movers of the era would doubtless have been
surprised at rumors disposed to group them as a school or sect,
and assuredly they would have been nonplussed over being dubbed
Transcendentalists, a name given nobody knows by whom, and
applied nobody knows just when.

The summer of 1839, writes W. H. Channing[1] in his " Memoirs,"
saw the full dawn of the Transcendental Movement in New England. " In part, it (the Transcendental Movement) was a reaction
against Puritan Orthodoxy; in part, an effect of renewed study
of the ancients, of Oriental Pantheists, of Plato and the Alexan-
drines, of Plutarch's Morals, Seneca and Epictetus; in part, the
natural product of the culture of the place and time. On the
somewhat stunted stock of Unitarianism, — whose dogma was
trust in individual reason as correlative to Supreme Wisdom, —
had been grafted German Idealism, as taught by masters of most
various schools, — by Kant and Jacobi, Fichte and Novalis,
Schelling and Hegel, Schleiermacher and De Wette, by Madame
de Staël, Cousin, Coleridge, and Carlyle; and the result was a
vague yet exalting conception of the godlike nature of the human
spirit."

The first evidence of the realization of what Transcendentalism
means, and of the acceptance of the term Transcendentalism —
with which their views were ascribed — by the Transcendentalists
themselves, we come across in the January number, 1842, of *The
Dial*. In a column entitled " Editor's Table " of this January
issue of *The Dial* we find the following significant statement:
" The more liberal thought of intelligent persons acquires a new
name in each period or community; and, in ours, by no very good
luck, as it sometimes appears to us, has been designated as Transcendentalism. We have every day occasion to remark its perfect

---

[1] Nephew of the great preacher, W. E. Channing.

identity, under whatever new phraseology or application to ne w facts, with the liberal thought of all men of a religious and con - templative habit in other times and countries."

Certain periodicals, of which *The Dial* is the most important, helped to promote from the very beginning the movement of Transcendentalism in New England. For the Transcendentalists were critics, " come-outers," from the old; and the journal, the periodical, became for a time of greater worth to them and more popular with them than the printed pages of books. Among the leading journals which were organs and interpreters of the liberal thought in New England in its incipient and later stages were: (1) *The Dial*, first published in Boston in 1840 by Weeks, Jordon and Company, and edited at first by Margaret Fuller and R. W. Emerson, with G. Ripley, H. D. Thoreau, and James Munroe as assistant editors; (2) *The Journal of Instruction*, first published in Philadelphia in 1833 by H. H. Porter, and edited by Wm. Rus- sell, A. B. Alcott, and Professor W. R. Johnson; (3) *The Christian Examiner*, edited at first (about 1834) by Dr. James Walker, Pro- fessor at Harvard College, and edited later (about 1857) by Dr. F. H. Hedge; (4) *The Plain Speaker*, published in Providence about 1841;[1] (5) *The Massachusetts Quarterly Review*, published in Boston under the editorship of Theodore Parker; and (6) *The Western Messenger*, published at Cincinnati and Louisville, but circulated to a large extent throughout New England, — J. F. Clarke and W. H. Channing, two New-England clergymen of the Uni- tarian faith, being the editors of *The Western Messenger*.

Some of the contributions to *The Dial*, the most important organ of New-England Transcendentalism, shadow forth in plain relief the nature of Transcendentalism in its beginnings in New Eng- land, and enable us to determine in a degree how the wind was then blowing. In his third " Lecture on the Times,"[2] in *The Dial*, January, 1843, Emerson says: " The first thing we have to say respecting what are called *new views* here in New England, at the present time, is that they are not new, but the very oldest of thoughts cast into mould of these new times. . . . The idealist, in

---

[1] See *The Dial*, July, 1841.
[2] The Transcendentalist, by R. W. Emerson, read at Masonic Temple in Boston in December, 1840; published in *The Dial*, Jan. no., 1843.

speaking of events, sees them as spirits. He does not deny the
sensuous fact; by no means; but he will not see that alone.   He
does not deny the presence of this table, this chair, and the wall
of this room, but he looks at these things as the reverse side of
the tapestry, as the other end, each being a sequel of completion
of a spiritual fact which merely concerns him. . . . The Transcendentalist adopts the whole connexion of spiritual doctrine.
He believes in miracle, in the perpetual openness of the human
mind to the new influx of light and power; he believes in inspiration and in ecstasy."

In a critical appreciation of a pamphlet [1] entitled " Transcendentalism," the reviewer writes somewhat effusively in the *The Dial*
(January, 1843) as follows: " Antecedent to all utterances, transcendent of all time, space, and motion, primal to spirit, originative
of soul, creative to body; everlasting, eternal, illimitable; in-
describable in any terms, these we use or other, — in the One, the
Underived, the Unit — God. . . . Most inquirers have like Locke,
limited themselves, and as far as they speculatively could, all
humanity to the bounds of intellect, asserting, with him, that
' the understanding is the highest faculty of the soul.' All who
have ventured affirmations from the higher level have been saluted
with epithets intended to be condemnatory, such as ' fantastic,'
' mystic,' ' theosopher,' and now, it seems, ' transcendentalist.' . . .
But the combination of a whole world of sensuous minds against one
transcendental soul will not move him. He is not an opponent to
them.   He sees all they see; he admits all their facts on their
ground, but this admission leaves untouched, unimpeached, that
other and higher class of facts, and that reality in being, which the
mere moral philosopher declares he knows not of, and the existence
of which he stoutly denies."

In an article entitled " Europe and European Books," [2] in the
April, 1843, number of *The Dial* we discover the following passage
apropos in particular of French writers: " Europe has lost weight
lately.   Our young men go thither in every ship, but not as in the
golden days. . . .   We remember when arriving in Paris, we
crossed the river on a brilliant morning, and at the bookshop of

---

[1] Boston, Crocker and Ruggles, 1842.
[2] Anonymous.

Papinot in the Rue de Sorbonne, at the gate of the University, purchased for two sous a Programme which announced that every Monday we might attend the lecture of Dumas on Chemistry at noon; at a half hour later either Villemain or Ampère on French Literature; at other hours Guizot on Modern History; Cousin on the Philosophy of Ancient History; . . . Prévost on Geology; . . . Jouffroy on the History of Modern Philosophy; . . . and Jouffroy on Greek Philosophy."

Three other articles in early numbers of *The Dial* refer explicitly to French philosophers and their writings. In the first — a critical review of " Channing's Translation of Jouffroy "[1] — we find these lines: " M. Jouffroy has been for some time very favorably known to our public. Few if any living writers upon Ethical Philosophy stand so high in the estimation of those who have made this science a study as he does." In the second — a critical appreciation of " Professor Walker's Vindication of Philosophy "[2] — we come upon this passage: " Authors of the best systems of philosophy have been accused of atheism, decried as dangerous, and exposed to the attacks of popular clamor. Descartes was called an atheist; Locke was called an atheist; Kant was called an atheist; and recently, the eminent French Eclectic, Cousin, has been called an atheist; in the latter case with as much propriety as in the former, and not a whit more." And the third article, found in the book review department of a later number of *The Dial*, relates to one of the translations of Cousin's Psychology: " When the following translation of a portion of M. Cousin's lectures was first published,[3] it was not supposed another edition would be wanted. A small edition, it was thought, might be disposed of among the few who took a special interest in philosophical studies. The work was, however, introduced into a number of our most respectable Universities and Colleges;[4] and the translator received repeated requests for a second edition, accompanied by very strong tes-

[1] *The Dial*, July, 1840.
[2] *The Dial*, October, 1840.
[3] Elements of Psychology, included in Critical Examination of Locke's Essay on the Human Understanding, with additional pieces by Victor Cousin, translated from French by Rev. C. S. Henry, D.D., N. Y., 1838.
[4] Prof. James Walker used it as a text-book with his classes at Harvard. Cf. Dr. Rand.

timonials to the value of the work. . . . He therefore determined some time ago to put out another edition. . . ."

The early stages of Transcendentalism in New England were marked not only by numerous utterances in periodicals, like *The Dial*, with strongly idealistic trend, but as well by numerous philosophical and literary assemblies and divers communistic associations.

The most distinguished literary association, known as the Transcendental Club,[1] and formed in the early enthusiastic days, we have previously mentioned. It was at first called the Symposium. The initial meeting of this particular organization was held September 19, 1836, at the house of George Ripley, then a Unitarian minister in Boston. The next meeting was held at the house of A. Bronson Alcott, 26 Front Street, Boston. There were sixteen members, all of more or less pronounced Transcendental tendencies. Their names are as follows:[2] Convers Francis, R. W. Emerson, A. B. Alcott, G. Ripley, F. H. Hedge, J. F. Clarke, C. A. Bartol, Margaret Fuller, Elizabeth P. Peabody, Theodore Parker, W. H. Channing, J. S. Dwight, Jones Very, H. D. Thoreau, R. Bartlett, Caleb Stetson. This group of men and women who met for the discussion of literature and philosophy constituted, as it were, from the beginning the storm-center of Transcendentalism in New England.

Among the chief communistic societies organized during the flood-tide of Transcendentalism in New England were *Brook Farm*, established at West Roxbury (1841–1847), and the *Fruitlands* community, founded almost contemporary with Brook Farm, at Harvard, near the town of Lancaster, Massachusetts. Both these associations bear witness to the French influence, especially that of the French Socialist, Fourier.

Most important of all the manifestations which accompanied the beginnings of Transcendentalism in New England for us, however, are the several translations of works of certain French philosophers which were neatly published in book form and widely circulated. George Ripley, in his " Specimens of Foreign

---

[1] The Transcendental Club, 1836–1850.
[2] For references see Memoirs of J. F. Clark, W. H. Channing, F. Sanborn; also G. W. Cooke on R. W. Emerson.

Standard Literature," [1] had published his translations of Cousin's
" Mélanges philosophiques " and Jouffroy's " Mélanges philoso-
phiques." W. H. Channing had published in two different
editions [2] his translation of Jouffroy's " Introduction to Ethics."
C. S. Henry had published in New York his translation of
Cousin's " Elements of Psychology." [3] H. G. Linberg published
in Boston in 1832 his version of Cousin's " Introduction of the
History of Philosophy." J. C. Daniel translated in 1849 Cousin's
" The Philosophy of the Beautiful." [4] The translation by O. W.
Wight of Cousin's " History of Modern Philosophy " was pub-
lished in New York, 1852. R. N. Toppan, in 1862, published a
version of Jouffroy's " Moral Philosophy." [5] Besides the above
seven there were two other somewhat unimportant publications, —
Sarah Austin's translation of Cousin's " The State of Public
Instruction in Prussia "; [6] and Mary L. Booth's translation of
Cousin's " Secret History of the French Court under Richelieu
and Mazarin." [7]

In the preface to his translation, H. G. Linberg writes concerning
Cousin a few words which are indicative of the temper of the time
toward Cousin, the renowned French Eclectic philosopher : " It
is well known that the lectures of M. Victor Cousin excite strong
emotions of sympathy and approbation, and are listened to and
read with that attention and respect which is the most satisfactory
evidence of a powerful conviction of their rationality and truth by
a very numerous class of intelligent and well informed young men
who may be fairly considered to represent the flower of the rising
generation in their respective countries." [8] And R. H. Toppan in the
preface to his edition writes as follows about Jouffroy : " The
following translation contains three extracts from the philosophical
writings of Jouffroy, one of the most profound of the French
philosophers of the nineteenth century and a pupil of the celebrated Cousin." [9]

[1] Hilliard, Gray & Co., Boston, 1838.
[2] James Munroe & Co., Boston, 1848; and Specimens of Foreign Standard
Literature, Hilliard, Gray & Co., Boston, 1840.
[3] Gould & Newman, N. Y., 1838.
[4] N. Y., 1849.   [5] W. H. Tinson, N. Y., 1862.
[6] N. Y., 1839.   [7] N. Y., 1859.
[8] Introduction to the History of Philosophy, W. H. Tinson, N. Y., 1862.
[9] Moral Philosophy, W. H. Tinson, N. Y., 1862.

Having given in a general way a definition of Transcendentalism, set forth a cursory sketch of miscellaneous precursors of the New-England movement, and outlined certain features which marked the beginnings of the Transcendental epoch in New England, we now come to the second part of our dissertation which comprises gathering together and setting forth some telling facts concerning the French Expositors of Transcendentalism.

II. FRENCH EXPOSITORS OF TRANSCENDENTALISM

1. Transmission of Transcendentalism into France

" FROM Descartes and Spinoza it (Transcendentalism) descended through Leibnitz and Kant, and their later interpreters, Cousin and Jouffroy," — so writes Mr. Johnson.[1] But other Frenchmen besides Cousin and Jouffroy were instrumental in taking up and carrying on the movement of Transcendentalism. Nine writers at least acted more or less the part of agents in developing in France the idealism of the later eighteenth and early nineteenth centuries; they are: Laromiguière, Royer-Collard, Maine de Biran, Degenerando, Guizot, Villiers, and Mme. de Staël, as well as Victor Cousin and Théodore Jouffroy.

France and Germany, indeed, in the early part of the nineteenth century, were the two great philosophical nations of Europe. The position of philosophy in these two countries, occupying the center of the European stage, is interesting. It marks an era of transition. With the close of the eighteenth century, Germany terminated an era of exclusive idealism, the idealism of Kant, Fichte, Hegel, Schelling; and France, taking up the idealistic movement where Germany laid it down, brought to a close an era of exclusive sensualism — the sensualism of the French Encyclopedists, Condillac, d'Holbach, and Helvétius.

The writers in France who especially helped to effect the transition from the exclusive sensualism of the eighteenth century school of philosophy to an eclectic idealism — of a German Transcendental sort — of the early nineteenth century are, — Laromiguière, who succeeded in separating the element of attention from sensation;

---

[1] Transcendentalism, S. Johnson, Boston, 1884.

Royer-Collard, who further undermined materialistic philosophy and introduced into France the incipient idealism of Scotch as well as German philosophy; Maine de Biran, who traced in an interesting way the origin of elevated ideas to human consciousness; Degenerando [1] who helped to bolster up, in his " Systemes compares de philosophie," the current idealistic theories; and, finally, the two distinguished philosophers, Cousin and Jouffroy, whom we have especially under consideration.

Several other figures in French literature are connected, in a minor way, with the idealistic movement in France which we have under consideration. Cabanis, who discussed systematically the relations of body and soul, is distinguished for being the predecessor of Laromiguière. Saint-Simon, the forerunner of Fourier, is regarded as the founder of French socialism of an idealistic, communistic nature. And then there are several French critics and philosophers who followed in the wake of Cousin and Jouffroy and are worthy of note in passing because of their sympathies and interests of a Transcendental sort, namely, Paul Janet, the author of a treatise on Plato; Barthélemy Saint-Hilaire, who made expositions of Aristotle's works and Hindu philosophy; Bouillet, the author of a dissertation on Plotinus; Émile Saisset, who discussed Spinoza; Tissot and Barni, who wrote upon Kant; and J. Simon and E. Vacherot, who were interested in the philosophic system of Cousin and undertook expositions of the Alexandrine School. But these figures either preceded or followed the main idealistic movement and are not directly connected with the transmission of Transcendentalism into France.

Madame de Staël was the first of the important French writers who were agents in transmitting German Transcendentalism into France. She traveled extensively in Germany during the years 1803–1804; wrote in her " De L'Allemagne," first published in 1810, critical appreciations of such German idealists as Wieland, the Schlegels, Fichte, Kant, and Jacobi; and even attempted in this volume cursory expositions of German philosophy in the chapters, — " De l'influence de la nouvelle philosophie sur le caractère des Allemands," " Des philosophes les plus célèbres de l'Allemagne,

---

[1] Mentioned by Cousin in Introduction to History of Philosophy, and by one of the editors of The Dial.

avant et après Kant," and " Du principe de la morale, dans la nouvelle philosophie allemande." [1]

We cite a selection or so, to illustrate the tenor of her writings bearing on German Transcendentalism, from her " La philosophie et la morale" in " De L'Allemagne " :

" Parmi les différentes branches de la philosophie, celle qui a particulièrement occupé les Allemands, c'est la métaphysique. Les objets qu'elle embrasse peuvent être divisés en trois classes. La première se rapporte au mystère de la création, c'est-à-dire à l'infini en toutes choses; la seconde à la formation des idées dans l'esprit humain; et la troisième à l'exercice de nos facultés, sans remonter à leur source. . . . Une foule de questions morales et religieuses dépendent de la manière dont on considère l'origine de la formation de nos idées. C'est surtout la diversité des systèmes à cet égard qui sépara les philosophes allemandes des philosophes français. . . . Il est donc impossible de faire connaître l'Allemagne, sans indiquer la marche de la philosophie, qui depuis Leibnitz jusqu'à nos jours n'a cessé d'exercer un si grand empire sur la république des lettres. . . . Je demandais un jour à Fichte, l'une des plus fortes têtes pensantes de l'Allemagne, s'il ne pouvait pas me dire sa morale, plutôt que sa métaphysique. ' L'une dépend de l'autre,' me répondit-il. Et ce mot était plein de profondeur; il renferme tous les motifs de l'intérêt qu'on peut prendre à la philosophie. . . . On s'est accoutumé à la considérer comme destructive de toutes les croyances du cœur; elle serait alors la véritable ennemie de l'homme; mais il n'en est point ainsi de la doctrine de Platon, ni de celle des Allemands; ils regardent le sentiment comme un fait, comme le fait primitif de l'âme, et la raison philosophique comme destinée seulement à rechercher la signification de ce fait." [2]

Victor Cousin, however, was a still more significant figure than Madame de Staël. In one of his lectures Schelling makes an interesting statement. He tells us: " In his different visits to Germany Cousin has won great personal esteem and friendship, not only among philosophers by profession, but among the German

---

[1] Cf. Œuvres complètes de Madame la Baronne de Staël, Holstein, Tome Deuxième, A Paris, Firmin-Didot Frères et Cie., 1836, first published in 1810.

[2] De L'Allemagne, Troisième partie, chapitre premier.

scholars in general. The peculiar circumstances which give the Germans a permanent interest in his labors is that he, together with the able and profoundly learned Guizot and a few others (Mme. de Staël, and M. Villiers in particular) was the first, after the restoration of peace from the wars of the Revolution, to awaken the attention of his countrymen to German science and literature. Cousin accomplished this particularly in regard to philosophy." He traveled in Germany in 1817, and again in 1824; and his divers lectures and writings bear abundant testimony to the fruitfulness of these visits. Cousin, moreover, following in the steps of his masters, Maine de Biran and Royer-Collard, helped to transmit the idealism of the Scotch philosophers of the later eighteenth century into France. He acted, indeed, as a kind of unifying factor, gathering to himself, assimilating, and recreating three phases of idealism which flourished simultaneously and with more or less distinctness in Europe along the latter part of the eighteenth century, — the German Transcendentalism of Kant and his followers; the Scotch idealism of Reid and Dugald-Stewart; and the incipient idealistic movement in France set afoot chiefly by such predecessors as Laromiguière, Maine de Biran, and Royer-Collard.

Madame de Staël, then, was the one to call the attention of Frenchmen to the German Transcendental philosophers, especially to Fichte and Jacobi. She was undoubtedly the first to become definitely acquainted with, and arouse widespread interest in France in German idealism, and in her remarkable volume — " De L'Allemagne " — she helped to bridge in a happy way the gulf in philosophy between the two countries. But her mission as a transmitter of Transcendentalism into France was of a cursory nature. It remained for Victor Cousin, and his disciple, Théodore Jouffroy, to develop the movement more extensively and thoroughly. They undertook investigations and expositions not only of the German philosophers but as well of the systems of Scotch and French idealists who came into vogue contemporary with the German Transcendentalists along the latter part of the eighteenth century. Cousin and Jouffroy, in short, developed, with a broad and proficient scholarship, the idealistic movement in France of the early nineteenth century, one phase of which — the introduction of German Transcendentalism — Madame de Staël successfully initiated.

2. Victor Cousin

Within sixty years, from 1760 to 1820, the source of philosophy in Europe underwent the changes of three distinct schools, — the Scottish, the German, the French. The leader of the Scottish School, which originated about 1760, was Reid. The German School, ascendant about 1790, arose out of the Transcendental philosophy of Kant and was highly developed by the German metaphysicians who succeeded him. The French School, inspired for the most part by the Germans, blossomed about 1820, with the idealistic, eclectic writings of Cousin and his disciple Jouffroy. All three schools were movements away from materialism in the direction of idealism, and all three represent successive stages of what is known as Transcendentalism. Victor Cousin, the principal exponent of French idealism of the early nineteenth century, and the most noteworthy French precursor of New-England Transcendentalism, although of humble origin, was yet a man of high education, profound learning, and wide travel.

" The philosophical merits of Cousin," writes George Ripley [1] the chief interpreter of Cousin in New England, " will probably not be new to the majority of the readers of these volumes. The translations which have been already made of two of his most important works [2] have contributed to give currency to his ideas, and in many cases to awaken a lively zeal for the study of the original. I may venture to say that there is no living philosopher who has a greater number of readers in this country, and none whose works have met with a more genuine sympathy, a more cordial recognition. He is destined, in my opinion, to exert an important influence on the development of thought, and the condition of philosophy in our youthful land." These words coming from George Ripley, who was one of the prime leaders of Transcendentalism in New England and most intimately acquainted

---

[1] Q. v. Preface to Specimens of Foreign Standard Literature, Vol. I, Hilliard, Gray & Co., Boston, 1838.

[2] (a) Introduction to the History of Philosophy, translated by H. G. Linberg, Boston, 1832.

(b) Elements of Psychology, translated by C. S. Henry, Hartford, 1834.

with the men of letters who formed with him the van of the Transcendental movement there, are significant.

Victor Cousin, the distinguished French philosopher who imbibed and recreated to such an extent the idealistic movement in philosophy of his time in Europe and helped conspicuously to pass it along to contemporaries in America, was born at Paris, November 28, 1792. Of lowly birth, a vagabond in Paris streets, he saved a rich lad from a pommeling in a fist fight; the wealthy darling's mother in gratitude rescued the fisticuff hero from the gutters of Paris, placed him in the Lycée Charlemagne, and helped him to become one of the prize scholars of the school. In 1810, at the age of eighteen, the brilliant young man entered the Normal School, which he never quitted after he was appointed head subsequent to the Revolution of 1830; he was appointed instructor in Literature at the close of the year 1812; and he was made Master of Conferences, in place of Villemain, in 1814. The life of philosophical achievement, from the beginning, absorbed him.

Cousin's philosophical knowledge in his early days as lecturer was not profound or extensive. He was dependent a deal for the little he had upon such masters in French philosophy as Maine de Biran, Royer-Collard, and Laromiguière. In his course at the École Normale the first year (1815–1816) he undertook to expound the Scottish philosophy of Reid and Dugald-Stewart, separating with clear analysis the good from the inferior in their system. The second year he with considerable success attacked and refuted the sensualistic doctrine of Condillac which was based on the empirical materialistic philosophy of Locke. He then continued along the lines of his predecessors, — in France, Maine de Biran and Royer-Collard, and in Germany, Kant, — developing the psychological as well as the Transcendental in his system. In 1822, when the Normal School was suppressed and Cousin in temporary disgrace, he traveled abroad to augment his learning and reputation. He made a tour of the German universities, large and small, interrogating not only philosophers but as well theologians. He met personally in friendly intercourse Goethe, Hegel, and Schleiermacher. At the sly instigation of a French Jesuit, he was arrested by the Prussian government on the charge of being a spy; but he deported himself during the disagreeable trial with such intelligent

— if not Transcendental — equanimity that his release was expedited and the German authorities were inspired with respect and admiration for him.

With the elections of 1827, the Villèle administration was overthrown, Royer-Collard was elected to the presidency, and Cousin was reëstablished as professor in the Faculty of the Normal School. He continued to lecture then, before enthusiastic bodies of students, till 1830, — his lectures being taken down word for word by stenographers, printed, and widely circulated. He passed, according to the strict forms of university promotion, from one of the Faculty of Literature in the Normal School to the royal council and principal direction of the institution. In order to provide a place for his ablest pupil, Jouffroy, he gave up to him the Chair of History of Modern Philosophy and assumed incumbency of the Chair of Ancient Philosophy. He constantly endeavored along idealistic lines to increase the prestige of the University. His energy, talents, and noteworthy services in the course of popular philosophy and belles-lettres finally led, after the death of Fourier, to his candidacy and election of the French Academy.

The following are the principal philosophical works of M. Cousin in the original arranged in chronological order : " Fragments philosophiques " (1826–1828), " Cours d'histoire de la philosophie " (1827–1840), " Cours d'histoire de la philosophie morale au XVIII siècle " (1840–1841), " Des pensées de Pascal " (1842), " Du vrai, du beau, et du bien " (1854), and, finally, " Histoire générale de la philosophie " (1864). One of the early American translators, however, C. S. Henry, gives us in his preface to his edition of Cousin [1] a somewhat more complete list of the early publications of the great eclectic philosopher, — an edition of " Proclus " in six volumes (1820–1827); an edition of " Descartes " in eleven volumes (1824–1826); " Philosophical Fragments," first edition, 1826, and second edition, 1833; " New Philosophical Fragments," 1828; " Introduction to the History of Philosophy," 1828; translation of " Tenneman's Manual of the History of Philosophy," 1829; " History of the Philosophy of the Eighteenth Century," 1829; works of Maine de Biran,

[1] Cousin, by C. S. Henry, Gould & Newman, N. Y., 1838.

Metaphysics of Aristotle, Scholastic Philosophy, and, finally, a translation of Plato with critical notes.

From these two catalogues of Cousin's works, the first from the New Century Cyclopedia and the other from the Preface to C. S. Henry's translation of Cousin, we see that there were already published during the flood-tide of Transcendentalism in New England at least nine of Cousin's works, namely: (1) the edition of "Proclus," (2) the edition of "Descartes," (3) the "Philosophical Fragments," (4) the "New Philosophical Fragments," (5) the "Introduction to the History of Philosophy," (6) the "Translation of Tenneman's Manual," (7) the "History of the Philosophy of the Eighteenth Century," (8) the "Course of Modern History," and (9) the "Moral Philosophy of the Eighteenth Century." And we find that of these nine at least five were, before 1842, translated, published, and widely circulated in New England, namely: three by George Ripley,[1] (1) "Preface to Tenneman's Manual," (2) "Preface to Philosophical Fragments," (3) "Preface to New Philosophical Fragments"; another by C. S. Henry,[2] (4) "History of Moral Philosophy of the Eighteenth Century"; and still another by H. G. Linberg,[3] (5) "Introduction to the History of Philosophy." It is worthy of mention, too, by the way, that in *The Dial* of October, 1840, there is an elaborate critical review of Cousin's "Cours d'histoire de la philosophie morale au XVIII siècle" and the "Œuvres complètes de Platon." It is, however, with the system of philosophy set forth in the five American translations of Cousin that we are chiefly concerned; for it is these works of Cousin which were read by the New-England Transcendentalists and which must have in no small measure furnished a basis for Transcendentalism in its early stages in New England.

Cousin's system of philosophy, as found in the five American translations, may be described as Eclecticism. It is eclectic in that it seeks to separate the best in all systems of philosophy and to construct with these choice selections a new perfect system. This eclectic method of Cousin is idealistic in tone, but it is not merely

---

[1] Hilliard, Gray & Co., Boston, 1838.
[2] Gould & Newman, N. Y., 1838. (See also earlier edition, Hartford, 1834.)
[3] Hilliard, Gray, Little & Wilkins, Boston, 1832.

idealistic, being characterized not a little by empiricist and rationalist methods and principles. It is not so poetic as Plato, nor so ingenious as Berkeley, nor so rigorously rational as Kant; but it combines in greater or less degree, with a peculiarly admirable and somewhat empirical order and precision, elements of Plato, Berkeley, and Kant.

The Middle Ages were subject to authority; everything was classified and controlled. The sixteenth and seventeenth centuries mark the inception of a new movement, the spirit of independence and the age of revolution. The eighteenth century is characterized by a spirit of scrutiny and analysis, as well as independence and development. Cousin passes in review the scholasticism of the Middle Ages, the philosophizings in the sixteenth and seventeenth centuries of Bacon and Descartes, and the principal systems in the eighteenth century of Locke, d'Holbach, Condillac; and the result of this examination of the course of philosophy Cousin tells us is the discovery of four distinct systems, namely: (1) Sensualism; (2) Skepticism; (3) Mysticism; (4) Idealism. The first, Sensualism, regards sensation as the sole principle of knowledge and reason. Skepticism, in its clearest form, notes the appearance of common sense on the scene of philosophy. Mysticism, on the other hand, designates a spirit the reverse of skepticism and allied to the symbolism and spiritualism of theology. Idealism, finally, takes as its point of departure from the reason of sensualism, the ideas or the laws infinite and eternal which govern its activity. The fact of the existence of these systems constitutes for Cousin an endorsement of their utility. They are useful in having helped to develop at a certain time a certain phase of human intelligence. They are also truthful in part, for absolute error is, according to Transcendentalism, inadmissible as regards human intelligence. It is the province of eclecticism, Cousin concludes, not absolutely to reject any one of them, nor to become the dupe of any one of them; but, by a discriminating criticism, to discern and accept the unalloyed truth in each.

In the "Preface to Tenneman's Outlines"[1] Cousin declares, illustrating his method of eclecticism, that modern philosophy can

---

[1] Preface to Translation of Tenneman's Outlines of History of Philosophy, q. v. Specimens of Foreign Standard Literature, G. Ripley, editor.

only take one of three courses: (1) Abdicate, renounce its independence, submit again to the ancient authority; or (2) continue its troubled motion in the circle of worn-out systems which mutually destroy each other; or (3) disengage what is true in each of these systems, and construct from the discriminated portions a philosophy superior to all systems. In the "Introduction to the History of Philosophy," [1] we come across another characteristic example of his eclectic method in a passage comparing Idealism and Sensualism: " You can neither abide by either of these two systems, nor escape from both. If, then, it has been proved on the one hand, that neither the one nor the other of these two systems can be regarded as the result of the last effort of the human mind, and if on the other hand, it has been also proved that not a single other system is given which is not reducible either to one or to the other of these two, what is to be done? Being thus hedged in by the necessity of either choosing between two opposite systems of which both are bad, or tormenting ourselves in vain to find a new system, which would nevertheless be either the one or the other of them more or less modified, we arrive, in extricating ourselves from this dilemma, at the only possible solution which yet remains, and which consists in the combination of these contrary systems, by rejecting all the exclusive views which we cannot admit, and by reconciling all the truths which they contain, which can be done only by regarding them in a point of view which, being more comprehensive than that of either the one or the other system, may be capable of including, and thus of explaining and completing them both."

Eclecticism is not, however, according to Cousin's own confession, a conception which belongs exclusively to himself. It did not originate yesterday. It was born the moment that a sound head and a feeling heart undertook to reconcile two passionate adversaries; it was long ago in the mind of Plato; and among the moderns it was not merely proposed by Leibnitz, it was constantly practised by him, and is everywhere presented in the rich historical views of the new German philosophy. The name Eclecticism, however, applied to this eclectic method in philosophy, originated with Cousin; and he and his disciple Jouffroy are generally referred

[1] H. G. Linberg translation, Boston, 1832.

to in text-books on philosophy as " the Eclectic Philosophers "
of France in the early nineteenth century.

The immediate predecessors of Cousin and his idealistic eclectic
philosophy were, as has already been pointed out, the idealistic
philosophers of the German, Scottish, and French schools of the
latter part of the eighteenth century. From Maine de Biran he
had his attention focused on the *activity* of the human mind, and
was led to separate it from circumstances, to analyze its character,
and to ascend to its original source in will; from Laromiguière he
got the phenomena of sensation cleared in his mind, and saw the
faculties of understanding and will referred to their ultimate
foundation; from Royer-Collard he was led to see in particular the
radical errors and hopeless limitations of the sensual philosophy,
and how new life and fresh interest could be imparted to familiar
truths. But Cousin, irrespective of the immediate influence of
such precursors in France as Maine de Biran and Laromiguière
and Royer-Collard, acknowledges especial indebtedness to Reid,
the Scotch idealist, and to Kant, the German Transcendentalist.
" Reid and Kant," he tells us, " in Scotland and Germany, have
fought to the death, and overthrown from top to bottom the
doctrine of Locke." [1] And again, after dividing in true Transcendental style the phenomena of consciousness into three classes, ne
writes: " This philosophy is represented in the philosophy of
the nineteenth century by the Scottish School; and especially by
the School of Kant, which, professing the same method, applies
it with far more rigor and completeness." [2] However much the
Scottish School of Reid and Dugald-Stewart or even his predecessors in France may have affected Cousin, the influence of the
German School assuredly preponderates. In the "Introduction
to the History of Philosophy " [3] our distinguished Eclectic writes:
" Kant is the true founder of rational psychology. . . . His cos-
mology and his philosophy of nature are nothing but a transfer
by induction of the subjective laws of thought into external nature."

[1] Preface to Philosophical Fragments, First Edition, 1826, G. Ripley translation, Boston, 1838.

[2] Philosophical Fragments, Second Edition, 1833, G. Ripley translation, Boston,
1838.

[3] Introduction to the History of Philosophy, H. G. Linberg translation, Boston,
1832.

And in the same volume he tells us, — "Fichte has, with greater consistency, gone further than his master (Kant). . . . In Fichte every object, being in respect to the subject nothing but what the subject causes it to be, is nothing but an induction of that subject, that is the subject itself, that is, the *me;* and thus the *me* is no longer considered merely as the measure, but as the principle of all things." And, finally, after personal acquaintance with Hegel and his lectures, Cousin confesses: "From our first conversation, I divined what he was, I comprehended his whole reach, I felt that I was in the presence of a superior man; and when I continued my journey from Heidelberg into other parts of Germany, I proclaimed him wherever I went; . . . his diction strong, but embarrassed; his countenance immovable; his brow covered with clouds, seemed the image of thought returning on itself."

The translation of the complete works of Plato, and the high regard professed for the personality and utterances of Hegel, plainly intimate the phases of philosophy to which Cousin is partial. In the American translations of his works, too, one finds that he makes frequent allusions, as the New England Transcendentalists do in their writings, to such philosophies of the East as the Vedas and the Bhagavad-Gita, to the Greek philosopher Aristotle as well as his teacher Plato, and to such philosophers of Transcendental bent in Germany, besides Fichte, Kant, and Hegel, as Leibnitz, Schlegel, Schelling, and Schleiermacher. One comes across also here and there isolated reference to such diverse figures with idealistic proclivity as Pythagoras, the Neo-Platonists, the English philosopher Bishop Berkeley, and the Dutch metaphysician Spinoza. Cousin, in short, is familiar with divers utterances bearing ear-marks of Transcendentalism in Hindu, Greek, German, and other sources. He is, along with these early philosophers, at the core more or less of a downright idealist, attaching importance to intuition, "immediate beholding," in the realms of philosophy, and disposed in general, as were his titanic Transcendental predecessors in Germany, to subordinate nature and experience to man, not man and nature to experience.

By means of citations from his writings let us attempt to set forth briefly the kernel of the Transcendental in Cousin. In the translation of "Introduction to the History of Philosophy,[1] we find such passages as these: " Inspiration is, in all languages, distinguished from reflection; it is the perception of truth without the intervention of volition and of individual personality. . . . The characteristic of inspiration is enthusiasm; it is accompanied with that forcible emotion which bears the soul away from its ordinary and subaltern state and disengages from it the sublime and godlike portion of its nature. The language of inspiration is poetry. . . . Spontaneity is the genius of humanity, as philosophy is the genius of some men. . . . Search in the history of languages, of societies, and of every remote epoch, and you will find nothing anterior to the lyric element, to hymns, to litanies. . . . Respect humanity in all its members; for in all its members there is a ray of divine intelligence and essential fraternity." And again illustrating in particular the eclectic spirit applied to idealism we quote from the same volume: " Idealism is that philosophy which, struck with the reality, the fecundity, and the independence of thought, of its laws, and of the ideas inherent in it, concentrates its attention upon these ideas alone, and beholds in them the principles of all things. Idealism is as true and just as necessary as empiricism. Without empiricism we should never have all that was continued in the bosom of sensation; and without idealism we should never have known the power properly belonging to thought."

In the "Elements of Psychology"[2] we come across other passages exemplifying elements of idealism in Cousin: " Enthusiasm is that spontaneous intuition of truth by reason, as independent as possible of the personality and of the senses, of induction and demonstration, a state which has been found true, legitimate, and founded upon the nature of human reason. But sometimes it happens that the senses and the personality which inspiration ought to surmount and reduce to silence, introduce themselves into the inspiration itself and mingle with it material, arbitrary, false, and ridiculous details. . . . Do not go to consult the savage, the child, or the idiot, to know whether they have the idea of God; ask them, or rather without asking them anything, ascertain if

[1] H. G. Linberg translation, Boston, 1832.
[2] C. S. Henry translation, Boston, 1838.

they have the idea of the imperfect and the finite; and if they have it, and they cannot but have it if they have the least perception, be sure that they have an obscure and confused idea of something infinite and perfect; be sure that what they discern of themselves and of the world does not suffice them, and that they at once humble and exalt themselves in a deep felt faith in the existence of something infinite and perfect."

And again, in the "Preface to Philosophical Fragments," [1] we happen upon such passages of a distinctly idealistic bent as the following: "The differences of individuals exhibit something noble and interesting, because they testify to the independence of each of us and separate man from nature. We are men and not stars; we have moments that are peculiar to ourselves; but all our movements however irregular in appearance, are accomplished within the circle of our nature, the two extremities of which are essentially similar. Spontaneity is the point of departure; reflection the point of return; the entire circumference is the intellectual life; the center is Absolute Intelligence which governs and explains the whole." In the same volume we also discover this explicit and significant statement: "In the recesses of consciousness, and at a depth to which Kant did not penetrate, under the apparent relativeness and subjectivity of the necessary principles of thought, I detected and unfolded the fact, instantaneous but real, of the spontaneous perception of truth, — a perception which, not reflecting itself immediately, passes without notice in the interior of consciousness, but is the actual basis of that which, at a subsequent period, in a logical form and in the hands of reflection, becomes a necessary conception." And once more, farther on in the same volume, we find these words: "Every man, if he knows himself, knows all the rest, nature and God at the same time with himself. Every man believes in his own existence, every man therefore believes in the existence of the world and of God; every man thinks, every man therefore thinks God, if we may so express it." Cousin's words have, in truth, in certain passages, the ring of Transcendentalism. He rigorously opposes the empiricist method of observation limited to the external world and sensibility alone, after the manner of Locke and Condillac; and stoutly

[1] First Edition, G. Ripley translation, Boston, 1838.

maintains along with Reid and Kant that human consciousness in itself constitutes the sure key to universal phenomena.

We conclude our exposition of the essence of Transcendentalism in the philosophy of Cousin by citing at random a few epigrams from miscellaneous sources in the American translations of his works:

"There is nothing intelligible but ideas."

"All things are in all things."

"Our negative ideas are secondary and logical.   Our primary ideas are positive and absolute."

"We do not commune with reflection, but with intuition."

"What has produced the *vision of God* of Malebranche, and the pre-established harmony of Leibnitz?"

"The field of philosophical observation is consciousness; there is no other."

"Every man, if he knows himself, knows all the rest, nature and God at the same time with himself."

"The human race, like the individual, lives only by faith."

"The first act of faith is the belief in the soul, and the last — the belief in God."

The merits of Cousin's Eclecticism stand out, at first sight, with more or less distinctness.   His philosophy evinces, from the first, abundant proof that it is the product of no ordinary thinker, but the utterance of an intelligence at once powerful and comprehensive, combining acute discernment and precise reasoning with command of language and facility in exposition.   His lectures render the most abstruse and difficult metaphysical problems at once, even to the average mind, clear.

A noteworthy writer for the *Edinburgh Review* testifies on behalf of Cousin: " He has consecrated his life and labors to philosophy, and to philosophy alone; nor has he approached the sanctuary with unwashed hands.   The editor of Proclus and of Descartes, the translator and interpreter of Plato, and the promised expositor of Kant, will not be accused of partiality in the choice of his pursuits while his two works, under the title of 'Philosophical Fragments,' bear ample evidence to the learning, elegance, and distinguished ability of their author."   And one of Cousin's contemporaries writes: " If it be true that Voltaire represented the spirit of the greater part of the higher orders in France, when he said that the success of Helvetius was not astonishing because he only told the secret of all the world, that is, of all the world at his day, it is but reasonable to conclude that the spirit of the well informed and intelligent young men in France, who at the present day idolize Cousin, is superior to the spirit presented by Voltaire, as the interior, intelligent, and dignified philosophy of Cousin is superior to the superficial, fanciful, and groveling sensualism of Helvetius."

The philosophy of Cousin, in short, establishes harmony between feeling and speculation, between emotional impulse and rational reflection. It listens to the voice of humanity, and succeeds in consummating a much needed union between religion and philosophy. It demolishes by lucid scientific analysis the materialism of Locke and Condillac with their unimaginative limitations. It builds up on the basis of intuitive faith a system of idealism akin to the world-great idealistic philosophies, expressing thoughts having the color of the thoughts of Plato, Plotinus, Proclus, Berkeley, Reid, Dugald-Stewart, Kant, Fichte, Hegel, Jacobi. Emphasizing the idea of universal harmony, reconciling the divorce between materialism and idealism, and being expressed, withal, in a grand literary style noteworthy for clearness, vigor, and grace, it is no wonder the Eclectic philosophy of Cousin tended to become for disciples in Europe and America a kind of laical religion, the religion of the enlightened spirits of the day.

The defects of Cousin's system seem to be threefold; it tends to the mediocre, the pretentious, and the sentimental. Eclecticism, being a kind of hodge-podge composition of the idealistic systems in Scotland, Germany, and France, respectively, of the latter part of the eighteenth century, must inevitably be less original and organic than the sources from which it was extracted. It appears to start, moreover, at the outset, with two fundamentally false hypotheses: (1) that all truths have already been expressed and only await clever eclectic editing; and (2) that the heterogeneous best in all philosophies can be excerpted and welded into a fresh and original perfect system. And, finally, after the manner of idealism in general, it manifests distinct partialities of its own and frequently errs on the side of the affectedly tender, — being disposed to depict in too rosy a hue the optimistic phases of social and human life, and to be too negligent of the various hard and cruel facts of nature and human experience. The Eclecticism of Cousin is, when all is said, a second class order of philosophy. It is a kind of critical and appreciative resumé of philosophy, not philosophy itself. It may be rated in the province of philosophy as opportunism is rated in the field of politics; it is in greater or less degree ingenious, but despite all, it is anomalous and more or less inefficient.

The spirit, rather than the contents of Cousin's system of Eclecticism, then, is what holds our interest and attention. The author's literary style is finished and brilliant; he sets forth high truths with regal sureness; he uplifts and fortifies the soul with fresh hope and confidence. We are, indeed, notwithstanding the somewhat amorphous and heterogeneous nature of the philosophy, not unseldom swept off our feet by it in bursts of sympathy and faith.

3. Théodore Jouffroy

The noted eclectic philosopher Jouffroy, referred to by one of the New-England Transcendentalists, W. H. Channing, as " one of the most profound French philosophers of the nineteenth century," was the disciple of Cousin, and, like his master, exerted considerable influence on the philosophy in France and the Transcendentalism in New England of his day. He was in character and temperament more grave, subjective, religious, even more fascinating, than his master, Cousin, but still less original, forceful, eloquent. He is distinguished not only for continuing, in the province of French philosophy of the Restoration Period, the work of the founder of the Eclectic School, but as well for enriching it with many profound and sincere refinements of thought and beauty.

Born five years after Cousin in Franche-Comté, of North Central France, Théodore Simon Jouffroy came to Paris when he was seventeen years old and entered in 1814 the *École Normale*. His parents were orthodox Christians who professed the ideas of 1789, and the young man was brought up inoculated with the views of the family. At the *École Normale*, studying under Laromiguière, Royer-Collard, and his senior contemporary Victor Cousin, Jouffroy found his religious sympathies to be irreconcilable with the principles of philosophy. He became for a time quite uneasy and melancholy; but his scientific consciousness triumphed in the end over certain religious tastes, and won for him the respect of fellow professors and pupils. In 1828 he was accorded, through the kind offices of Cousin, a course in " Ancient Philosophy " in the *Faculté* of the Normal School; and in 1830, at the age of thirty-four, he was appointed Professor of History of Modern Philosophy and Master of Conferences. Two years later, in 1832, he was elected Professor of Greek and Latin Philosophy at the *Collége de France;* and, after 1838, acted as Librarian of the University.

Jouffroy went, not like his master, Cousin, from philosophy to faith, but the inverse, from faith to philosophy. He seems never to have become wholly reconciled to losing the peace of religion; and the slight note of dolorous austerity in his writings is due in no small measure to religious sentiments left unsatisfied in his make-up. Despairing of pushing philosophy into the domains of orthodoxy, he naturally fell back on the self-contemplative and psychological processes which Cousin enjoined. His utterances, however, resound from first to last with a fervor and a tenderness to which Cousin, his master, never attained; we were, says Renan, charmed by Cousin's eloquence; but by Jouffroy's simplicity of emotion and moral grandeur we were inebriated.

The writings of Jouffroy are considerably less numerous than those of Cousin. His first works of importance were " Translations " of the Scottish philosophers, Reid and Dugald-Stewart. Later he published at intervals the following volumes : " Mélanges philosophiques " (1833), " Nouveaux Mélanges " (1842), "Cours de droit naturel," 3 vols. (1835–1842), and, finally, " Cours d'esthétique (1843). The lectures on " Introduction to Ethics," which came out in the " Mélanges philosophiques," were the first which Jouffroy had published. At the earnest request of the students who had attended his first course he consented to have them, when they were given again, taken down by a stenographer. They set forth many choice thoughts of an idealistic flavor; some of the grand problems of human destiny; a review of various systems of ethics; and certain fundamental principles of morality which Jouffroy himself, in an eclectic spirit, draws from various systems of ethics.

Of the various writings in the original from Jouffroy, we have, under different titles, at least seven noteworthy American translations: two by George Ripley in " Specimens of Foreign Standard Literature,"[1] namely: " Preface to Translation of Dugald-Stewart " and " Philosophical Miscellanies "; two by William H. Channing from different publishers, — " Critical Survey of Moral Systems "[2] and " Introduction to Ethics ";[3] and, finally, three by Robert N. Toppan: " Problem of Human Destiny," " Moral Facts of Human Nature," and " Theoretical Views."[4] These translations from the original of Jouffroy amount in bulk to more than the translations from the original of Cousin. It may be interesting to remark too, in passing, that Dr. James Walker, professor of philosophy at Harvard, used in his classes from 1840 to 1850, as text-book to accompany some of his philosophical lectures, Jouffroy's " Introduction to Ethics." The philosophy of Jouffroy as set forth in the American translations must have influenced most our Transcendentalists of New England, as was the case with the American translations of Cousin; and so it is with the philosophy advanced in these just enumerated translations that we are chiefly concerned.

Jouffroy and Cousin, one should note by the way, although influenced in general by the same precursors of German, Scotch, and French origin, were yet influenced respectively in different degrees by different writers among these precursors. Cousin was particularly indebted to his fellow-countryman Maine de Biran (1766–1824) who traced the origin of elevated ideas to human consciousness and presented to France a new and more spiritual philosophy. Cousin was also in large measure indebted for philosophic principles to the German Transcendentalists, especially to Fichte, Kant,

[1] Hilliard, Gray & Co., Boston, 1838.
[2] Hilliard, Gray & Co., Boston, 1840.
[3] James Munroe & Co. (2 vols.), Boston, 1845.
[4] W. H. Tinson, N. Y., 1862.

and Hegel, and was influenced in an appreciably less degree by the Scottish idealists Reid and Dugald-Stewart. Jouffroy, on the other hand, was particularly influenced by the ideas of Maine de Biran's colleague, Laromiguière (1756–1837), who reacted strongly against materialism and skilfully referred the human faculties of understanding and will to their ultimate foundation. Jouffroy, moreover, although somewhat acquainted with idealism in Germany of the late eighteenth and early nineteenth centuries was a deal more intimately acquainted not only with the Scottish idealism of Reid (1710–1796) and Dugald-Stewart (1753–1828) but as well with the philosophies of their English contemporaries Cudworth and Price. A discerning investigator, on the alert for distinctions, may, indeed, plainly detect in the writings of Jouffroy beyond what may be detected in the writings of Cousin, ear-marks of the influence of Laromiguière rather than Maine de Biran and of Scottish and English rather than German idealistic philosophers. Both Cousin and Jouffroy, however, were wide readers in the province of philosophy, and were, as Eclectics, primarily systematic expounders of the philosophies of others, rather than creators of new philosophies of their own. To give an inkling of the variety and range of their learning, and at the same time a cue to their distinctly circumscribed eclectic spirit, we cite a passage from Jouffroy's lecture on the " History of Philosophy " [1] (1827): " When we think of the powerful minds, from Pythagoras to the present day, which have wrought in every part of the fields of philosophy; above all, when we run through the admirable monuments of their researches; . . . we can hardly avoid conviction . . . that all the facts of human nature and philosophy have been perceived and noted, and that it is difficult, if not impossible, to fall upon a new idea or fact of importance." Let us now turn to a consideration of the philosophy in general of this French Eclectic as set forth in the several American translations.

The lecture entitled " Introduction to Ethics," in which Jouffroy undertakes a critical review of various ethical systems, is remarkable for its wide research, scrupulous observation, and lucidity of expression. It is analytical and methodical almost to a fault. It determines with acumen upon the main issues in systems of ethics,

[1] Q. v. Mélanges philosophiques, 1833.

is on the whole sane if somewhat partial in judgment of them, and uniformly accords due deference to good points in a system while sifting out errors. Through the luminous and well-regulated mind of Jouffroy, indeed, many a reader of his writings in New England was introduced for the first time, from an idealist's viewpoint, to the ethical principles of Hobbes, Bentham, Smith, Price, and others, and enabled to weigh them in the balance arranged and classified with admirable skill.

In the lecture on " Philosophy and Common Sense " [1] we note, among other things, Jouffroy's capacity for eclectic synthesis going hand in hand with superb French rationality. He tells us in this lecture that we are always likely to find the solution of common sense more comprehensive than abstruse philosophical solutions. He shows himself to be appreciative of such practical philosophers as Zeno, the Stoic, who defined good as that which is in accordance with reason; as Epicurus, the founder of an austere Hedonism, who defined good as agreeable sensation; and as the German critic of pure reason, Kant, who defined as good that which is obligatory. Common sense, according to Jouffroy, adopts all these opinions, and yet is committed to none of them. The exclusive spiritualists, our idealistic yet circumspect Eclectic continues, affirm the existence of spirit; the exclusive materialists affirm the existence of matter; and the one ends with denying matter, and the other with denying spirit. But common sense equally admits both matter and spirit and thus places itself in some measure in contradiction to each of these systems and at the same time in some measure in agreement with them. The empiricists, like Locke, recognize no source of knowledge as authentic but the senses; Descartes admits none but consciousness; Plato and Kant are disposed to make reason and conception predominate over that which can be attained by the senses or consciousness. Common sense, or in other words, nineteenth century Eclecticism, acknowledges the authority of consciousness, of senses, and of reason. And, Jouffroy adds, if we pursue the parallel in regard to other questions, we shall always find the same result.

Jouffroy, like his master and contemporary Cousin, is indeed a lucid, although cautious, systematizer. In his " Facts of Man's

[1] *Q. v.* Ripley's Specimens of Foreign Standard Literature, Boston, 1838.

Moral Nature"[1] we come across a characteristic example of his proficiency along this line: " It is long since the common sense of humanity has declared that man sustains in this life four principal relations: the *first*, to God; the *second*, to himself; the *third*, to things, animate and inanimate, which people the creation; the *fourth*, to his kind. Through all ages, therefore, the inquiry has been, what are the rules for human conduct in these four grand relations; and the science of ethics has been divided into four corresponding branches." The four grand relations are, according to Jouffroy, man's relation to (1) God, Religion; (2) Self, Mysticism; (3) Things, Pantheism; and (4) Fellows, Humanism. Let us consider briefly, then, some of Jouffroy's views concerning these principal relations.

Under the division, Man's Relation to God, he assures us that from the moment an organized being begins to exist its nature tends to the end for which it is destined, viz., good, or God. " As soon as man exists, his nature aspires, in virtue of his organization, to the end for which he is destined, through impulses carrying him on irresistibly towards it. . . . When reason first begins to exert its power, it finds human nature in full development, its tendencies all in play, and its faculties active. In virtue of its nature, that is to say, of its power of comprehension, it enters into the meaning of surrounding phenomena, and it at once comprehends that all these tendencies and faculties are seeking one common end, a final and complete end, which is the satisfaction of our entire nature. . . . Toward this good all passions of every kind aspire; and it is this good (God) which our nature is impelled, with every unfolding faculty, to seek." To the student of the history of philosophy this passage alone, concerning man's relation to God, reveals at once what an adept idealistic eclectic Jouffroy is. We discern in it certain fundamental ideas of Plato, Aristotle, Fichte, Kant, and others, skilfully appropriated and fused into a new order.

The discussion of the division, Man's Relation to Himself, Mysticism, is equally pointed and interesting. It is the chief tenet of mysticism, Jouffroy informs us, that the human mind can, through contemplation, arrive at an understanding of truth and

[1] W. H. Channing translation, Boston, 1840.

actual being, of which it is quite incapable in its ordinary condition, and can thus hold communion with the future, with unseen spirits, with God Himself. The most perfect symbol of mysticism is the anchorite who conceived the idea of living upon the top of a column,[1] and who passed long years there in total inactivity. Every system, Jouffroy continues, in true eclectic manner, has some truth for its foundation. Man cannot without some absorption of his faculties in contemplation attain the highest good, and that degree of good which is accessible, that complete destiny which his nature promises, must be gained by painful effort, by earnest self-imposed self-restraint. But Jouffroy sanely concludes that the consequences which the mystics deduce from this are false. It is in becoming a person that we become a cause, a free intelligent cause, having an end and plan and responsibility for acts, — in a word, something like to God. The state of being a kind of watch, endowed with sensation, and enjoying passively the pleasure of feeling within it the operation of unimpeded movements, is scarcely comparable as a prototype course of conduct to that of being an active moral and rational agent, a man.

The third grand relation, Man's Relation to Things, Pantheism, Jouffroy expounds in the following manner. He first intimates in a general way that pantheism is the doctrine that the universe with its multitudinous forces and laws is God. He then passes on to a consideration of the philosophic system of Spinoza who is, broadly speaking, the chief pantheist in modern philosophy. But almost at the outset of his discussion of Spinoza, Jouffroy retrenches a bit in characteristically cautious fashion; he assures us the belief that the universe is God, and that God is the only universe Spinoza himself earnestly repels. The essence of God, according to Jouffroy in interpreting Spinoza, is existence, and His necessary desire is to remain existence. As an emanation from God, the human soul participates in the fundamental desire of God, and also aspires to a continuance of existence, as a created being. And, finally, Jouffroy tells us, in the course of his eclectic construction of pantheism, that nothing can be more proper, more consonant with reason, than the end to which our desire and passions tend. This end, somewhat as our end in relation to God, is the greatest degree

---

[1] Simeon Stylites — the Syrian ascetic (died 459 A. D.).

of real existence, the highest perfection of our being. All that we can do to attain this end is lawful and right, and the pursuit of it is virtue. Thus knowledge, existence, real being, perfection, virtue, happiness, are all the same thing under different aspects.

The fourth grand relation, Man's Relation to his Fellow Beings, Humanism, our ingenious Eclectic breaks up, in his customary systematic way, into four sub-divisions, namely: (a) Skepticism, (b) Egoism, (c) Sentimentalism, and (d) Rationalism. We find these four sub-divisions of Humanism most clearly set forth in another one of W. H. Channing's translations under the title, "Critical Survey of Moral Systems." [1]

Skepticism, as one would naturally suppose, elicits little favor from Jouffroy. He regards this doubting system as offering a form of amusement to the man of talents, but as unworthy to divert the attention of the philosopher. Under his refutation of skepticism, however, he writes in a somewhat unusual and strictly psychological vein: "There is not, and cannot be, in human intelligence, any elementary notion which is not derived either from observation of what actually is, by the senses and consciousness, or from the conceptions of what must be, by the reason. And here an important remark should be made — reason never rises to the ideas which it is her function to introduce into human knowledge, unless the communications of observations first supply the occasion." We may discern in this terse sizing up of the situation an adroit attempt to reconcile the tenets of empiricism with those of idealism.

The sanity with which Jouffroy lays before us the second sub-division of humanism, the main points of Hobbes' self-interest philosophy, and then, with a few masterly touches, punctures the heart of it, is interesting. "Hobbes declares that self-interest is the sole motive of human choice. He asserts that the end of every action is the pursuit of pleasure or the escape from pain. . . . If I desire the possession of a certain object as necessary to my well-being, my neighbor may consider it necessary to his, and may look upon my act of taking possession as injurious to him. Hence inevitable contests, . . . What then," in the mind of Hobbes, "is the end of society? The repression of the state of war." Then Jouffroy quietly and incisively tells us, in opposition to

[1] Hilliard, Gray & Co., Boston, 1840.

Hobbes' selfish system and with a view to silencing it: "If we never obeyed the tendencies of our nature, except from the considerations of the pleasure that will accompany their gratification, then would it be impossible that we should ever act at all. For, plainly, we should never know that the gratification of desires would procure us pleasure, except by having once experienced this pleasure." Amusing, too, is the superb way in which Jouffroy disposes of Bentham, an exponent along with Hobbes of the selfish system: "I honor the men who are called practical, and am perfectly aware of their merits. . . . Practical men admit only those faculties in a man whose effects they can appreciate. They make much of a good stomach, of strong limbs, of the five natural senses. . . . But as to faculties more refined and elevated in nature, they either despise them, or deny their existence. . . . Bentham, gentlemen, belonged to this class that I have now described; and he had all the energy and enterprise, all the sagacity and confidence, which characterizes practical men. . . . The fundamental hypothesis of the selfish system admitted and professed as it has been in similar terms by Epicurus, Helvetius, Hobbes, and all advocates of the system, without exception, could not be more clearly expressed. . . . It might be said," Jouffroy concludes, "that the selfish motive does not even offer a reason for acting. . . . Shall I or shall I not act? This is the practical question to be settled. Self-love answers, act, because your nature demands it. That this may be a reason, it is necessary that it should express an evident truth; but so far is this from being evident, that reason at once demands its proof. If I am satisfied with the reply of self-love, I obey not a reason, but a natural desire. As a matter of fact, then, the follower of interest acts not from reason, but from passion." And thus Jouffroy points out how in the attempt to explain and justify the selfish principle we escape from its control.

Sentimentalism and rationalism are, according to Jouffroy, the two characteristics by which the systems professing to be disinterested and the systems professing to be interested may be distinguished and classified. He begins with an exposition and criticism of the philosophy of an advocate of the sentimental system, Smith the Scottish philosopher.

Justice is a duty, according to Jouffroy's way of construing Smith, the sentimental philosopher, because others have the right to compel us to observe it. " Whence comes their right? From the fact that injustice would do them a positive wrong! My only *duty*, then, is not to injure others; my only right is to prevent their injuring me. I violate *duty* whenever I do evil to a fellow-being; he violates my right whenever he does an evil to me." Jouffroy then asks, in plain terms, who would admit such propositions? " Who would allow that they coincide with the true ideas of duty and right?" He refers here and there in his discussion of the sentimental system to Jacobi and German idealists, as well as to the Scottish School, and shows how France has had little to do with promoting this system: Condillac and Helvetius, anything but sentimentalists, represent the logical outcome of this sort of speculation in France.

Jouffroy's words on Mackintosh, the English moralist, another sentimentalist, are also interesting. " Mackintosh believes in the reality of disinterested volitions, and denies that reason is capable either of assigning any end for conduct, or of exerting any influence over the will. . . . Moral conscience is a sensible principle. . . . This principle is not primitive; it is created and developed, as he thinks, gradually; or, to use his expression, it is a secondary formation." But reason, according to the sentimentalists, is capable of deciding what is good or what is bad for man; therefore moral distinctions cannot emanate from it, but must inevitably emanate from instinct. Jouffroy then avers in a mediatorial fashion that — " Reason does not lead man in one direction, self-love in another, and instinct in a third; but, on the contrary, self-love, when enlightened, counsels us to pursue the very course to which instinctive desire impels, and reason, as the moral faculty, prescribes what self-love thus advises."

Having examined in a general way the solutions of the moral problem as given by the skeptical, selfish, and sentimental schools, Jouffroy undertakes at last a review of the systems which seek the rule of human conduct where he himself believes it is most truly to be found — in the conceptions of reason.

At an early day, Cudworth maintained rationalistic opinions in opposition to the system of Hobbes. Cudworth, says Jouffroy, taught that our ideas of good and of evil are not communicated either by sense or experience. Reason is the vital factor; it instantly conceives the ideas of good and of evil, from a contemplation of human actions, and as absolutely as it conceives the ideas of cause from that of events, or the idea of space from that of bodies. " Whence come these ideas which we find within us ? From the divine mind, which is their natural and eternal home, and from which human reason is an emanation." We recognize in this system the doctrine which Plato so admirably unfolded. The system of Price, Jouffroy next takes up and proceeds with like a master. " Ideas communicated by the intelligent faculty denote realities which are independent of ourselves, and which would exist if we were otherwise constituted, and even if we ceased to be. The ideas communicated by the sensitive faculties, on the other hand, denote only inward facts and sensations, which would not exist without us, and would change if we were changed." But, Jouffroy adds, intellect cannot explain certain ideas, because, in the first place, these ideas represent nothing which can be observed either within or without us; and, because, secondly, they represent that which transcends the bounds of all observation, and of all generalization; in other words these ideas are absolute. " If we should analyze the truths which in any nation or time the common sense possesses we should find that they are composed of two elements: first, of a few innate articles of faith, which are in some sort the intellectual capital, received at birth as a gift from God to all men; and secondly, of numberless truths, which successively acquired by reflection through preceding generations have gradually become a part of this common stock." The intellect, then, appears under two forms, — first as *a priori* intellect, or intuitive reason, which conceives of an invisible that transcends all observation and all experience; and second, as *empirical intellect*, or understanding, which sees in things such qualities as can be observed. According to Cudworth, Price, Dugald-Stewart, and other noted exponents of the rationalistic system, the idea of good is only an idea of a quality in actions recognized by intuitive reason. But Jouffroy says in his circumspect eclectic fashion, by way of concluding the discussion of the rational system, that moral good is not an intrinsic attribute of certain actions, as a round form

4

is of certain bodies, it is a relation existing between actions and
an end, absolutely good in itself, to which these actions may or may
not be directed, and by relation to which they are good when they
tend toward it, and bad when they do not.

Although throughout Jouffroy's writings there is a tinge of melancholy austerity, although he is patently a lover of orderly arrange-
ment and logical sequence of ideas, the element of personal force
now and then stands out distinctly in his utterances. In Toppan's
translation of the lecture entitled, " On the Faculties of the Human
Soul," [1] we note a ringing passage with elements quite akin to Transcendentalism : " Personal life," Jouffroy tells us, " is nothing but
the fatiguing struggle of man or liberty, against the world or necessity; and as the personal power cannot destroy the necessary current of external phenomena, nor prevent it from soliciting our
faculties, it must do two things in order to govern them; that is,
restrain them when they wish to obey solicitations which address
them, and fix them on the particular subject to which it attempts
to apply them. . . . To combine all the energy of a capacity on
a single point, to restrain it there for some length of time, — this is
the effect of the action of the personal power on our faculties.
Hence the prodigious efficiency of a strong will; hence the miracles of attention and the miracles of patience which have suggested
the remark that genius itself is nothing but unwearied persever-
ance." And then follows a passage, supplementing the personal
power note, and illustrating the inexorable, common-sense element, with slightly optimistic flavor, never long absent from
Jouffroy's writings, — " To meet with obstacles is the characteristic of the human condition. . . . If happiness should come
before merit, there would never be any possibility either of virtue
or morality arising. . . . The present life is, therefore, pre-
eminently good, because it is preëminently bad. Its excellence
is in the evil it contains; for the price of this evil is morality, is
personality."

Jouffroy resorts so often to such phraseology as *firstly, secondly,
thirdly,* he employs so frequently such connectives as *thus, therefore, however,* and what not, that — confronted so persistently with
this formal technique — we may sometimes have good cause to

[1] W. H. Tinson, N. Y., 1862.

doubt whether such a rhetorician is at heart a Transcendentalist. Certain lines from one of Toppan's translations [1] ought to dispel at once from our minds any misgivings on this score. The accomplishment of our end or of our good, and the accomplishment of the end or the good of other beings is, according to Jouffroy, our duty, the moral law. It arises " from a certain number of truths *a priori*, which, in making their appearance in our understanding, illuminate the creation with a searchlight, reveal the meaning of it, solve the problem and unfold its law. Experience excites in us the manifestation of these truths, but it does not produce them; they exist *a priori*, and they are, therefore, universal, absolute, necessarily conceived." The Transcendental note in these lines is in truth so obvious as to bear striking resemblance to the tenor of Kant's thoughts concerning the categorical imperative.

Jouffroy was, we know, an Eclectic. He seized here and there upon the quintessence of philosophy in philosophy and set it forth in fresh form in his own writings. Let us, then, conclude our exposition of his Eclecticism with a few excerpts, of a noteworthy Transcendental trend, from his lectures in the various American translations:

"By an irresistible tendency, thought arises from individual to social order, from social to human order, from human to universal order. Universal order supposes a universal maker, of whom it is at once the thought and work. Human intelligence then ascends even to God, and there it finally rests, because there it finally discovers the source of that immense stream which the inflexible logic of principles governing it obliges it to ascend."

"High as is my respect for the popular mind, I yet think this popular mind rather fitted to recognize truth than to discover it; of all the great truths which have influenced the destinies of the human race, I know not one which originated in the instinct of the mass; they have all been the discoveries of gifted individuals, and the fruit of the solitary meditations of thinking men."

"Truth is order conceived, as beauty is order realized. In other words, absolute truth, the perfect truth, which we imagine in the Deity, and of which we only possess fragments in ourselves — is not, and cannot be,

---

[1] Theoretical Views.

anything more than the eternal laws of that order which all things tend to fulfil, and all rational beings are bound voluntarily to advance."

"Our capacities are ours, but are not ourselves; our nature is ours, but is not ourselves; that alone is ourselves which takes possession of our nature and of our capacities, and which makes them ours; we are found entirely in the power which we have of mastering ourselves; it is the action of this power which constitutes our personality."

"There is no contradiction between faith and skepticism; for man believes by instinct and doubts by reason."

Jouffroy did not seek in philosophy merely the origin and nature of ethical ideas and the nature in general of the human understanding. He made, as well, philosophical inquiries about God and his works, about the universe and its ends, about death and the hereafter; and he troubled his spirit a deal to arrive at right conclusions concerning these problems. Jouffroy manifests in the course of his investigations above all else two distinctive qualities, — fineness of observation and clearness of reasoning. And these two qualities enabled him, under all circumstances, broadly speaking, to analyse with acumen and infer with sureness.

With his power of observation and proficiency in generalization, Jouffroy distinguishes carefully in man the spiritual from the vital principles which are the main objects of the two sciences — psychology and physiology. He shadows forth, too, quite distinctly the simple spiritual being in the midst of natural phenomena; and then, by means of subtle analysis, proves reason to be the bond between the spiritual and material in man. The moral in the social order, according to Jouffroy, is simply the law of conduct in consonance with the ends of human nature and human reason.

Jouffroy evinces in his make-up, from beginning to end, a deal of the artist and man of religion as well as the idealistic and ethical eclectic philosopher. He sees in the beautiful a religious phase of the good; and he perceives in justice and sympathy a moral side. The truth, to him, is order in thought; the good is order in conduct; the beautiful order in form. These religious and artistic conceptions he brings out especially happily in his "Cours de droit naturel" and in his doctrines "d'Esthétique."

Jouffroy is not only a remarkable thinker, he is also a gracious and, at times, even a brilliant writer. He had, as his utterances plainly show, integrity of spirit, elevation of mind, fineness of feeling, analytical acumen. Although not particularly powerful as a philosophical lecturer and writer, he yet expresses himself with unusual distinction. There is in his utterances, indeed, a certain intangible modesty, sage reticence, delicate forthcoming of a noble soul, that invests what he says with a charm beyond and above what could be achieved by mere power.

But Jouffroy, like his predecessor, Cousin, errs somewhat on the side of the superficial. He undertakes almost too wide a survey in the province of philosophy; touches too generally only on the summits in systems of ethics; descends too infrequently to specific details. He undoubtedly had the genius for drawing up orderly expositions and effecting clever generalizations; but he had not the genius for organic and consistent synthesis. He not unseldom is swayed in one lecture toward idealism, and in another toward materialism, and always he manifests a slight bent toward an orthodox monism.

It is evident that he vaguely respected the word science and enjoyed the exercise of pure reason; but the exercise of inexorable rationality concerning problems in philosophy was almost as alien to him as it was to Amiel. He appears to have been perpetually a prey to conscientious misgivings.

Jouffroy, in short, seems always to have felt it more or less necessary to doubt, — to doubt the validity of psychological ethics apart from religious sensibility, and to doubt the validity of religious sensibility apart from psychological ethics. He never, however, in his chief utterances, departs widely from a discreet psychological standpoint. He is in certain respects in the field of philosophy, like his contemporary and colleague, Cousin, too much inclined to be a mediator, a moderator, an opportunist. He has the merits and the defects of the eclectic philosophers in particular and the system of nineteenth-century eclecticism in general.

4. Transcendentalism in French Dress

In the course of the development of philosophy in France in the nineteenth century, at the time when the Transcendental philosophy of Kant and his followers was beginning to have vogue, one may almost invariably detect a note of order and a consecutiveness standing forth throughout the process of development. Rationalism, more or less humanistic and utilitarian in nature, seems indeed to constitute from first to last — despite idealistic, Transcendental, or whatever other tendencies in the air — the keynote of French philosophy. This element of rationalism, at all events, appears to be conspicuously present in the idealistic philosophy in France of the early nineteenth century, — the eclectic philosophy of the Restoration Period.

There are discernible, too, in the philosophy of France in the later eighteenth and early nineteenth centuries, two kinds of rationalism; they might be described respectively as naturalistic rationalism and as ethical rationalism. The first order, more or less impractical, is embodied in the sentimental philosophy of Rousseau and his various disciples. The other order, savoring more of the normal and practical, is well set forth in the psychological philosophy of Royer-Collard and Maine de Biran. Both these orders tend to slide into one, blended with the Transcendental philosophy current in France at the time, in the compromise philosophy of the Eclectics — Cousin and Jouffroy. And the eclectic philosophy of Cousin and Jouffroy, under the influence of French civilization, appears gradually to slide off into the somewhat abnormal, socialistic, and utilitarian philosophy of the French philanthropist, Fourier.

Philibert Damiron tells us in a characteristically orderly and consecutive French way, in his exposition of French philosophy,[1] that there were in France during the first decennia of the nineteenth century three schools, (1) the Sensualistic, (2) the Theological, and (3) the Spiritualistic Schools. This intelligent classification of Damiron is in a general sense, skilfully adopted and developed by Paul Janet, a pupil of Cousin, in the essay entitled " Le Spiritualisme français ou xix siècle."[2]

Janet declares, in brief, that philosophy in France at the end of the Revolution and at the beginning of the nineteenth century was entirely dominated by the Sensationalistic School of philosophy,

[1] Ph. Damiron, Essais sur l'histoire de la philosophie en France au XIX siècle, Paris, 1828.
[2] Q. v. Revue des Deux Mondes, vol. 75, 1868, pp. 353-385.

the philosophy of Condillac; the physiological Condillacism was represented by Cabanis (1757–1808), and the ideological Condillacism was represented by De Tracy (1754–1836). Then there naturally set in a reaction against the Sensationalistic, or Sensualistic, School. The reactionary faction is known as the Theological School: De Bonald (1754–1840), the first of the theologians, declared revelation to be the principle of all knowledge; the Abbé de Lamennais (1782–1854) is notable as the chief advocate of theological skepticism in the nineteenth century; and Joseph de Maistre (1753–1821), dreamed of a vast religious renovation, and is reputed the founder of modern Ultramontanism. And, finally, there came into being, the Spiritualistic, or Psychological School, which was entirely independent of theology; sought in psychology the principles of ethics and theology; and incarnated, withal, in some measure, the modern Transcendental tendencies of Kant.

The Psychological School, which we have already discussed at considerable length, was at first represented by Royer-Collard (1766–1824), and later by the French Eclectics, Victor Cousin, and his disciple, Théodore Jouffroy. But the idealistic psychological Eclecticism of Cousin and Jouffroy is simply an orderly and logical outcome of the philosophy in France immediately preceding. A careful analysis of nineteenth century French Eclecticism clearly shows, indeed, in greater or less degree, elements of the prior Sensualistic, Theological, and Spiritualistic Schools, — intermixed more or less with certain exotic elements of Scotch Idealism and German Transcendentalism.

The organization of institutions of higher learning in France, in the early nineteenth century, opened for philosophers brilliant careers of letters and helped to accentuate the idealistic and rationalistic tendencies in French philosophy. Among the most noteworthy of the men who held professorships of philosophy in the universities were the French Eclectics, Cousin and Jouffroy. In describing these two distinguished exponents of idealistic rationalism in France in the nineteenth century, one writer says of Victor Cousin, " tempérament imaginatif, passionnait l'histoire de la philosophie par de vives allusions que l'auditoire saissait au vol. Il déroulait tous les systèmes, et l'infini, en belles phrases harmonieuses et nobles, parfois élégamment nuageuses; il inventait l'éclect-isme, et coulait doucement dans le panthéisme." And in describ-ing Jouffroy, the same writer tells us: "Jouffroy, disciple de Cousin, et tout le contraire de Cousin: grave, sobre, précis, intéri-eur, contenant son émotion, détaché du christianisme avec angoisse, et reconquérant douloureusement les grandes vérités chrétiennes par la philosophie, il recherchait, avec une sincérité et une réelle force de pensée, le problème de la destinée humaine, ou posait les principes du droit naturel et de l'esthétique."[1]

These lines describing Cousin and Jouffroy hint of another trait of French character which should be mentioned along with the national trait of rationalism, namely, amenity. The French race, in truth, is preëminently civilized, urbanized. Vivacity, graciousness, quickness of wit are proverbial among French men and women of letters. A style rhetorical and impassioned, based on the *terra firma* of good sense, and tending in spirit and content to adapt philosophy to the world rather than the world to phi-losophy, is quite generally characteristic of French philosophers. Transcendentalism in French dress, then, is to be found dis-tinguished not only by rationalism, but as well in no small degree by amenity. A few lines from the writings of Cousin bear for us on this score significant witness: "L'art qui recherche et discerne le vrai dans les différents systèmes; qui, sans dissimuler ses justes préférences pour quelques uns, au lieu de se complaire à condamner et à proscrire les autres à cause de leurs inévitables erreurs, s'ap-plique plutôt, en les expliquant et en les justifiant, à leur faire une place légitime dans la grande cité de la philosophie, cet art élevé et délicat s'appelle l'éclectisme. Il se compose d'intelligence, d'équité, de bienveillance. Il est la muse qui doit présider à une histoire vraiment philosophique de la philosophie, et c'est celle-là que nous invoquons."[2]

The decline in French philosophy of the first half of the nine-teenth century is marked by the wane of idealism, rationalism, and amenity. Rigorous and ethical and urbane idealism gradually tapers off into a crude order of utilitarianism. The eclectic phi-losophy of Cousin and Jouffroy, more or less ingrained with

---

[1] G. Lanson, Histoire de la Littérature française, Paris, 1898.
[2] Q. v. Cousin, Histoire générale de la philosophie, 1re leçon, 1829.

elements of Transcendentalism, winds up, in short, with the hedonistic socialism of Fourier.

François Charles Marie Fourier (1772–1837), the notable French socialist and contemporary of the nineteenth century French Eclectics, was born, as was Jouffroy, in Franche-Comté. His father was an affluent draper, and the son received a somewhat liberal education at the college of his native town. On completing school education, he traveled for some time in France, Germany, and Holland. On the death of his father, he inherited considerable property which enabled him to live for a time in leisure; but this inherited wealth was shortly swept away during the French Revolution. Fourier then entered the army; but after two years of service he was discharged on account of ill health. About this time he began to publish articles on European politics, attracting some little attention. In early middle life he entered a merchant's office in Lyons, and a few years later he undertook on his own responsibility a small business as broker. He obtained from these employments just sufficient means and leisure to enable him to elaborate his works [1] on the reorganization of society. His theories of social reorganization, more or less characteristic of French genius, and more or less influential on the Transcendentalists of New England, are worthy of brief consideration.

Fourierism, like the schemes of socialists in general, is the creed of a man who feels more strongly than he reasons. But Fourierism differs materially from other systems of socialism and communism. Civilization to-day, Fourier taught, is in a crude and infantile stage; the poverty, crime, ignorance, misery, vice around us spring from unnatural restraints imposed by society on the gratification of desire.[2] It the desires or passions of men, their aptitudes and inclinations, could be allowed freer scope, they would, Fourier argues, infallibly produce, instead of discord, harmony, — the highest condition and greatest happiness of which they are capable.

Harmony, Fourier claims — from his peculiarly idealistic and decidedly socialistic viewpoint — is to be found throughout the universe in its four great departments, — society, animal life,

---

[1] Théorie des Quatre Mouvements, Lyons, 1808; Traité d'association domestique agricole, Paris, 1822; Le nouveau monde industriel, Besançon, 1829; La fausse industrie morcelée, Paris, 1835.   [2] Cf. Rousseau.

organic life, and the material world.[1]   God is the center of the harmony and from Him all things flow. So, seeing and believing that all things from suns and planets to ants and atoms come from God and range themselves in orderly groups and series, according to certain fixed laws of attraction and repulsion, Fourier labored to set forth a scheme of human society that would be in conformity to these laws.

Society, in Fourier's plan, is to be divided into departments or *phalanges*, each *phalange* numbering about sixteen hundred or eighteen hundred persons. Each *phalange* group inhabits a *phalanstère*, or common building, and has a certain number of acres of soil allotted to it for cultivation; and as adjuncts to the group life there are to be shops and studios, as well as farms, — all appliances, in short, of industry and art and as well various sources of education, amusement, pleasure. The property of the association is to be held in shares; and the apartments of the big central edifice, the phalanstère, are to be of various prices. ,The staple industry of the *phalange* is, of course, to be agriculture; and the menial work of the association is to be done by children who love dirt and are thus as it were naturally fitted for the office of scavengers. The institution of marriage is to be abolished and an ingeniously constructed régime of free love substituted. (It is best, however, to pass over in silence and neglect, as did the New-England Transcendentalists, the teachings of Fourier on the question of family life.) The twelve passions of the human soul, — the five sensitive: sense, hearing, taste, sight, touch; the four affective: friendship, love, ambition, paternity; and the three distributive: emulative, alternating, composite, — are to be given free scope. These Fourier deems to be the true motive forces of society. Emulation, in particular, the desire of success, honors, rewards, he believes should be relied on as the great stimulant to elicit exertion. When we come to the chapter on *The Brook Farm Community* of the New-England Transcendentalists a few other phases of Fourierism, not mentioned here, can be brought out.

The objections to this somewhat crude and highfalutin order of socialism are, of course, patent. It appears to make — as did

[1] Cf. Plotinus's Emanatistic Pantheism. Bakewell, Source Book in Ancient Philosophy, N. Y., 1907.

the hedonistic philosophy of Epicurus — luxury, ambition, and sensual delights the end of existence. The theory of license in relations between the sexes if put into practice would be liable to lead to ruinous chaos. The whole creed from first to last leaves too much out of consideration the factors of wide-ranging individual initiative, wholesome human self-interest, and enlightened common sense.

The French socialistic philosopher Fourier we find, in short, was all through life of a very retiring and sensitive disposition. He appears, one cannot help thinking, to have mingled so little in society as to have remained in large part in ignorance of real human nature and of sane social arrangements; the strangeness of some of his acts and theories, indeed, almost warrants one in believing that there were in his make-up elements of insanity. His socialistic creed is not especially interesting or important in itself. It is, however, more or less significant for us as a vital phase — along with the Eclecticism of Cousin and Jouffroy — of the philosophy which was developed in France and transmitted to New England during the first half of the nineteenth century, and which helped to constitute here the source of some of the ideas of New-England Transcendentalism.

III. RELATION OF NEW-ENGLAND TRAN-
SCENDENTALISTS TO FRENCH
PHILOSOPHERS

1. GEORGE RIPLEY

THE outburst of Transcendentalism in New England seems to
have received inspiration in large measure from without —
from Oriental and Occidental literature, particularly from the
philosophy of the French Eclectics of the early nineteenth century
— and partly from within — from certain phases of preceding
American literature, such for instance as the writings of the philosophical clergyman, William Ellery Channing, and from the
hearts and consciousness of the New-England Transcendentalists
themselves.

The Transcendental Movement in New England appears, moreover, to have flourished by a noteworthy coincidence almost simul-
taneous with the Romantic Movement of Germany in the latter
part of the eighteenth and early nineteenth centuries of which
Goethe and Richte are significant figures; with the Romantic
Movement of England in the latter part of the eighteenth and the
early part of the nineteenth centuries of which Wordsworth and
Coleridge are the principal exponents; and with the Romantic
Movement of France in the early nineteenth century of which at
first Madame de Staël and Chateaubriand, and later in the realm
of philosophy of the Restoration Period the French Eclectic
philosophers, Cousin and Jouffroy, are noteworthy representa-
tives. An indefinable something, like electricity, appears, indeed,
to have been astir in the intellectual and spiritual atmosphere of
New England, as well as in England, France, and Germany, about
the beginning of the nineteenth century.

Transcendentalism in New England is commonly associated with the name of Emerson. He was, however, simply the finest and best fruit of the whole era. Other figures in the course of the movement, especially as regards the relation of French philosophers to New-England Transcendentalism, are quite as important as Emerson.

The two great Unitarian clergymen in New England in the early nineteenth century, William Ellery Channing and Theodore Parker, men of wide learning and true inspiration, were — we must note in passing — distinctly instrumental from the beginning in setting afoot in our midst the Transcendental Movement. Channing,[1] for instance, gives among others as the sources of his inspiration such philosophers and men of letters as Swedenborg, Madame de Staël, Reid, Dugald-Stewart, Price, Goethe, Schleiermacher, Wordsworth, Coleridge, Carlyle, and often definitely refers to Cousin's translation of "Plato" and "Introduction to Ethics" as well as to Jouffroy's writing in general. Parker, Channing's successor as chief Unitarian clergyman in New England, mentions, we find, in his "A Discourse on Religion,"[2] his "Discourses on Theology," and his "Theism, Atheism, and Popular Theology," Cousin several times and the "Eclectic Philosophy of modern France" more than once, along with such familiar figures as Plato, Swedenborg, Böhme, Kant, Fichte, Schelling, Hegel, Reid, Stewart, Wordsworth, Coleridge, and Carlyle.

But the chief editors of *The Dial*, Ralph Waldo Emerson and Margaret Fuller, and the prime movers of the *Brook Farm* and *Fruitlands* experiments, George Ripley and Amos Bronson Alcott, should we believe be generally regarded nowadays as the leading lights of the Transcendental movement of the early nineteenth century in New England. Let us, then, undertake briefly a general survey of the lives and utterances of these figures with a view to getting an insight into the characteristics of their Transcendental writings and an inkling in general into the nature of their relation to the eclectic philosophers of the early nineteenth century in France — Cousin and Jouffroy.

[1] Cf. Reminiscences of Rev. Wm. Ellery Channing, D.D., by Elizabeth Palmer Peabody, Roberts Bros., Boston, 1880.
[2] Cf. Works of Theodore Parker, Trubner & Co., London, 1876.

George Ripley was undoubtedly one of the leading lights among the Transcendentalists of New England as regards love of philosophy and extent of learning. The two French philosophers, Cousin and Jouffroy, who exerted such marked influence on the idealists in New England in the early part of the nineteenth century, he translates himself and edits with elaborate introductory and critical notes in his *magnum opus* in fourteen volumes entitled " Specimens of Foreign Standard Literature." No New-England man of letters of the early nineteenth century is more Transcendental in spirit, evinces more scholarly devotion to the advancement of philosophy, or shows more patently interest in the French Eclectics and admiration for them than this figure among the New-England Transcendentalists of whose life and writings we undertake first a brief review.

Ripley, who may be aptly called the man of letters of the New-England Transcendental Movement, was born at Greenfield, Massachusetts, October 3, 1802. He graduated from Harvard College in 1823, and remained there a year or so after graduation as an instructor. On leaving College he turned to theology, and graduated in 1826 from the Cambridge Divinity School. Thereafter for five years, from 1826 to 1831, he was pastor of a Unitarian church in Boston.

All through life he was ever busying himself with philosophical speculation and social reform. Gradually and inevitably he was drawn into the Transcendental circle; wrote on metaphysics and education; and lent his influence to promoting knowledge of Continental Literature, — sojourning several years in Europe in order better to accomplish his purpose.

He was, too, one of the prime movers of the Brook Farm socialistic experiment. And between 1840 and 1841 he was associated with Margaret Fuller and Emerson in conducting *The Dial.* He contributed articles to the *Christian Examiner;* was one of the editors of the *Harbinger;* and, in 1842, when the Brook Farm community broke up, he went to New York where he became literary editor of the *New York Tribune,* remaining such until his death.

The most important piece of work in the province of literature, however, which Ripley undertook on his own initiative and completed in the course of his lifetime, was that of editing the "Specimens of Foreign Standard Literature." It was published in parts by Hilliard, Gray and Company of Boston. Volumes I and II of the series, containing philosophical miscellanies from the French of Cousin and Jouffroy — translated and edited with critical notes by George Ripley himself — were first printed in 1838.[1] The relation of Ripley to French philosophers centers chiefly about the translations of the French Eclectics, Cousin and Jouffroy, set forth in these volumes.

As the frontispiece of volume I a selection is quoted from Milton's "History of Briton." It runs as follows: " As wine and oil are imported to us from abroad, so must ripe understanding, and many civil virtues, be imported into our minds from foreign writings; we shall else miscarry still, and come short in the attempt of any great enterprise." We might, by a stretch of the imagination, infer that if George Ripley had in mind any " great enterprise " it was the dissemination throughout his country of the ideas of Transcendentalism, and that the introduction of the writings of foreign philosophers into our midst he intended as a means of assisting to carry out successfully his mission.

His preface as editor of the volumes is interesting and illuminating. We set forth a few telling passages: " The design of issuing a series of translations from the works of several of the most celebrated authors in the higher departments of modern German and French literature, has already been announced by the Editor of these volumes. . . . Among the writers, from whom it is proposed to give translations, are Cousin, Jouffroy, Guizot, and Benjamin Constant, in French; and Herder, Schiller, Goethe, Wieland, Lessing, Jacobi, Fichte, Schelling, Richter, Novalis, Uhland, Korner, Holtz, Menzel, Schleiermacher . . . in German." The catalogue of French and German writers cited, apprises us, in some measure, of the breadth of Ripley's erudition in French and German literature. It also adduces invaluable information for those in search of sources of inspiration of the New-England Transcendentalists.

Of the fourteen volumes comprising George Ripley's "Specimens of Foreign Standard Literature," five are devoted to French

[1] Hilliard, Gray & Co., Boston, 1838.

writers, — one to Victor Cousin, two to Théodore Jouffroy, one to Benjamin Constant, and one to Guizot. Insomuch as the latter two, Constant and Guizot, rank in the realm of world literature rather as critics and historians than as idealistic philosophers, we have deemed it fitting to eliminate at the outset their writings from consideration. Three volumes with ear-marks of Transcendentalism remain then in the "Specimens of Foreign Standard Literature" devoted to the writings of French philosophers; and these three volumes, being the first published and among the most widely circulated, constitute a significant, although not large, element.

Ripley selected from Cousin's philosophical writings for translation and editing in the "Specimens of Foreign Standard Literature" the following,[1] — "Preface to Tenneman's Manual," "Preface to Philosophical Fragments," and "Preface to New Philosophical Fragments"; and he translated and edited from Jouffroy two pieces of writing, namely, — "Preface to Translation of Dugald-Stewart" and "Philosophical Miscellanies." He also secured the services of William H. Channing in the work of translating and editing from the writings of Jouffroy the following,[2] — "Critical Survey of Moral Systems" and "Introduction to Ethics." It is interesting to recall here, by the way, what we found to be in general the nature of the writings of Cousin and Jouffroy selected by Ripley and his associate Channing for translation and editing in the "Specimens of Foreign Standard Literature."

Ripley concludes the Editor's Preface to his *magnum opus* with a paragraph — coming from a Transcendentalist — remarkable for its catholicity of taste and scholarly discretion. He writes: "As this work ("Specimens of Foreign Standard Literature"), if continued, will be composed of the contributions of different translators, entirely independent of each other, it is proper here to state that it is devoted to the advocacy of no exclusive opinions; that it is designed to include works and authors of the most opposite character, without favor or prejudice; and that no individual is responsible for any sentiment or expression that it may contain, which does not proceed from his own pen."

[1] *Q. v.* Specimens of Foreign Standard Literature, Vol. I, Hilliard, Gray & Co., Boston, 1838.
[2] *Q. v.* Specimens of Foreign Standard Literature, Vols. II and III, Hilliard Gray & Co., Boston, 1838.

The merits in general of George Ripley, one of the most active, earnest, and influential figures of New-England Transcendentalism, are worthy of at least cursory mention. He was a scholar, a linguist, a hard worker. He had a large library, good taste, was well versed in theology, philosophy, and literature. He became, in the natural course of events, one of the chief mediums through which the ideas and sentiments of the French and German Transcendentalists found their way into the life and literature of New England.

Religious in sentiment Ripley was to the core of his being. His best-known writings remaining to us — the " Discourses on the Philosophy of Religion " — are, for the most part, concerned with earnest and able theological discussion and exposition. In them he manifests the optimism and idealism characteristic of the Transcendentalists of New England. The tone of these writings, indeed, is more than hopeful and idealistic: it is scrupulously conscientious, after the manner of Jouffroy. A deal of feeling is evinced; but it is, as was Jouffroy's, fairly well under the control of intellect.

Optimistically religious in sentiment, Ripley was naturally somewhat disposed toward philanthropy. He had, like the French Eclectics, Cousin and Jouffroy, an abiding faith in the intuitions of the soul, and the soul's assurance of the permanent possibility of increasing good. He would mitigate the sin and misery of the world; bridge the gulf between the affluent and the penurious; and spread more generally throughout the world enlightenment, prosperity, godliness.

Of the Brook Farm socialistic experiment, established at West Roxbury, he was one of the prime leaders. He bravely renounced social success and conventional respectability; and generously surrendered himself to the sway of this idealistic scheme for the institution of a Utopia on the soil of Massachusetts. The principles of the French socialist, Charles Fourier, formed the basis — along with the idealistic and psychological philosophy of Cousin, Jouffroy, and others — upon which most of his visionary theories were built. We quote a significant passage from *The Constitution* of the Brook Farm Association of which George Ripley was such a prominent and potent factor, —

" In order more effectually to promote the great purpose of

human culture; to establish the external relations of life on a basis
of wisdom and purity; to apply the principles of justice and love
to our social organization in accordance with the laws of Divine
Providence; to establish a system of brotherly coöperation for
one of selfish competition; to secure to our children and those who
may be entrusted to our care the benefit of highest physical, intellectual, and moral education, which in the progress of knowledge
the resources at our command will permit; to institute an attrac-
tive, efficient, and productive system of industry; to prevent the
exercise of worldly anxiety, by the competent supply of our necessary wants; to diminish the desire of excessive accumulation, by
making the acquisition of individual property subservient to upright and disinterested uses; to guarantee to each other forever
the means of physical support, and of spiritual progress; and thus
to impart a greater freedom, simplicity, truthfulness, refinement,
and moral dignity, to our mode of life. . . ."

Such is the nature of a phase of purest and truest Transcendentalism in New England. And it was largely owing to the tireless
energy, indomitable will, and the unfaltering hopefulness of Ripley
that the community, founded on this constitution having a somewhat French hue, lasted the length of time that it did, — six
years.

Another significant passage from the writings of Ripley which
combines idealism of a virile sort with faith in an inner light, all
in the interests of social reform, is from the pages of *The Harbinger*, — the journal of the Brook Farm community. It runs as
follows:

" We shall suffer no attachment to literature, no taste for abstract discussion, no love of purely intellectual theories, to seduce
us from our devotion to the cause of the oppressed, the down-
trodden, the insulted and injured masses of our fellow-men. Every
pulsation of our being vibrates in sympathy with the wrongs of
the toiling millions; and every wise effort for the speedy enfran-
chisement will find in us resolute and indomitable advocates. If
any imagine from the literary tone of the preceding remarks that
we are indifferent to the radical movement for the benefit of the
masses which is the crowning glory of the nineteenth century, they
will soon discover their egregious mistake. To that movement,

consecrated by religious principle, sustained by an awful sense of justice, and cheered by the brightest hopes of future good; all our powers, talents, and attainments are devoted."

The general tone of this manifesto seems somewhat deficient in amenity, — noble in purpose as it is. As we read it, we may be reminded of the character of Hollingsworth, drawn by Hawthorne in " The Blithedale Romance "; and we can scarcely help thinking that there may be after all considerable resemblance between the iron-minded hero of that novel and the actual George Ripley.

A leader and an organizer of men Ripley assuredly was. The preacher spirit, a common accompaniment of rulership, was, too, apparently strong in his make-up. He believed in the testimony of the soul above the external senses; was hopeful of a better state of things; and was inclined, in a practical way, to try to realize in every-day life the ideal. But it is plain, notwithstanding his divers merits, that he did not possess that fineness of fibre and delicacy of sentiment, that strength of thought and poise of mind, characteristic of his compeer — Emerson.

2. MARGARET FULLER

Sarah Margaret Fuller, the contemporary of Ripley and Emerson, may well be called the critic of the Transcendental Era in New England. As the relationship of Ripley to the French philosophers — Cousin and Jouffroy — centers chiefly about his renditions of their writings in the " Specimens of Foreign Standard Literature," so the relationship of Margaret Fuller to the French Eclectics resides principally in her editing of *The Dial*. Both Margaret Fuller and Ripley were downright idealists; were allied by bonds of sympathy and interests to the Transcendental movement in New England in all its phases; and were keenly alive to the importance of contemporary foreign literature of an idealistic trend, especially that of France and Germany, and were instrumental in getting it at least in part gathered together and set before the New-England public of their day.

The various letters and essays of Margaret Fuller clearly evince her whole-souled allegiance to the idealistic movement which characterized the time and place in which she lived. She writes in one of her epistles: " Every noble scheme, every poetic manifestation, prophesies to man his eventual destiny. And were not man ever more sanguine than facts at the moment justify, he would remain torpid, or be sunk in sensuality. It is on this ground that I sympathize with what is called the ' Transcendental Party,' and I feel their aim to be the true one." And later on she continues somewhat plaintively yet in a quite level-headed vein: " My position as a woman, and the many private duties which have filled my life, have prevented my thinking deeply on several of the great subjects which these friends (the New-England Transcendentalists) have at heart."

This remarkable woman of letters, the critic of the Transcendental Era in New England, was assuredly strenuously educated. She was the eldest child of Timothy Fuller, a hard-working lawyer and congressman of Cambridgeport, Massachusetts; and at various times in her life the care of the younger brood devolved heavily on her. At the age of six she began Latin, and at the age of thirteen Greek, and she permanently impaired her health by this and other early application. On the death of her father, in 1835, she undertook the support of her younger brothers and sisters by public and private teaching.

All through life she was distinguished by violent emotions and intellectual eccentricities. She was ever an ardent and conspicuous literary figure, associated in the realm of American letters with such men as Emerson, Hawthorne, Thoreau, and Dr. Channing. In 1837 she became principal of a school in Providence, Rhode Island. In 1840 she assumed the editorship of the famous organ of New-England Transcendentalism, the quarterly magazine called *The Dial.* In 1844 she removed to New York, on invitation of Horace Greeley, and became there under him for a time literary critic of *The Tribune.* She was particularly interested in the *Brook Farm* experiment, at West Roxbury, and was a frequent guest there; although, like Emerson and Hawthorne, she never committed herself to its enthusiastic vagaries.

In middle life came the crisis of her career. It was at this time, about 1846, that she went to Europe where her eager personality led her into association, as it had in America, with various social, political, and literary leaders. And then at Rome, in 1847, she met and married Giovanni Angelo, Marquis d'Ossoli, by whom she had one child. In the Italian struggle for independence, which ensued shortly after her marriage, she took an active part, and served heroically during the French siege of Rome as directress in one of the hospitals. On the capture of the city she took refuge first in the mountains of Abruzzi, and then at Florence. In May, 1850, she embarked with her husband and child at Leghorn for the United States. The vessel on which she sailed was wrecked in a gale off the shore of Fire Island just outside New York; the child's body was found on the beach, but nothing was seen afterward of the mother or the father.

The Dial,[1] the famous organ of New-England Transcendentalism, and for being editor of which Margaret Fuller is chiefly noted, grew out of conversations held at homes of Transcendentalists in Boston and Concord. "Several talks among the Transcendentalists during the autumn of 1839," writes W. H. Channing, "turned upon the propriety of establishing an organ for the expression of freer views than the conservative journals were ready to welcome. The result was the publication of *The Dial*, the first number of which appeared early in the summer of 1840, under the editorship of Margaret Fuller aided by R. W. Emerson and George Ripley." It was issued quarterly for four years, from July, 1840, to April, 1844. Margaret Fuller and R. W. Emerson were editors-in-chief, and George Ripley, H. D. Thoreau, and James Munroe were assistant editors. Weeks, Jordon, and Company, 121 Washington Street, Boston, and Wiley and Putnam, 67 Paternoster Row, London, were the respective publishers. All its papers were unpaid contributions, the work of mutual aspiration and mutual admiration, — its regular contributors being its chief readers. Mr. Sanborn compiles the following list as the chief contributors to *The Dial*: "the Channings, Ellery and William Henry — nephews of the great preacher, the Sturgis sisters, Ellen and Caroline, Elizabeth Hoar, betrothed to Charles Emerson, Margaret Fuller, Henry Thoreau, S. G. Ward, Freeman Clarke

---

[1] See article on *The Dial*, by George Willis Cooke, *Journal of Speculative Philosophy*, July, 1885.

and his artist-sister, Allston's pupil, George Bradford, Theodore Parker, Elizabeth Peabody, Ednah Littlehale, Robert Bartlett and Marston Watson of Plymouth, and later James Lowell and George William Curtis — these and many more, older or younger, as years advanced, came into the circle." [1]

Of this Quarterly Journal,[2] issued in Janaury, April, July, and October, from July, 1840, to April, 1844, we have sixteen numbers. In these sixteen numbers we find no less than five distinct and significant references to the French philosophers whom we have under consideration. In the issue of July, 1840, we find an elaborate critical appreciation of William H. Channing's "Translation of Jouffroy"; in the issue of October, 1840, we find a book review of Professor James Walker's "Vindication of Philosophy," in which the name of Cousin figures conspicuously; in the edition of October, 1841, there is a book review of George Ripley's "Specimens of Foreign Standard Literature," the first three or four volumes of which are devoted to translations of Cousin and Jouffroy; in the same edition, too, there are brief book notices of Cousin's "Cours d'Histoire de la Philosophie Morale" and his "Œuvres complètes de Platon"; and, finally, in the number of July, 1842, there is a long article on "Fourier and the Socialists." The matter in these just mentioned references is not especially worthy of reëxposition; it consists, for the most part, merely of cursory appreciations, flying comments, brief book-review notes. It is sufficient to indicate, however, on the part of the various New-England Transcendentalists connected with the circulation of *The Dial*, definite acquaintance with the French Eclectics, Cousin and Jouffroy, and marked interest in their published works, both in the original and in translation.

Margaret Fuller was the editor-in-chief of *The Dial*. An editor, we know, determines to a large extent the tone of a paper's columns. Let us then, with a view to getting at the sort of literature Margaret Fuller and her co-editors favored, examine the nature and tone of some of the more striking articles published in their periodical.

[1] See Ralph Waldo Emerson, by Frank Sanborn, Small, Maynard & Co., Boston, 1901.
[2] See The two-volume edition of *The Dial*, collected and edited by the Harvard College Library.

An article entitled " Lecture on the Times " in the July, 1842, number of *The Dial* contains some significant passages: " The reason and influence of wealth, the aspect of philosophy and religion, and the tendencies which have acquired the name of Transcendentalism in Old and New England; the aspect of poetry, as the exponent and interpretation of these things; [1] the fuller development and freer play of character as a social and political agent; — these and other related topics will in turn come to be considered. . . . There is no place or institution so poor and withered, but if a new strong man could be born into it, he would immediately redeem and replace it.[2] . . . As the granite comes to the surface, and towers into the highest mountains, and, if we dig down, we find it below the superficial strata, so in all the details of our domestic or civil life is hidden the elementary reality, which ever and anon comes to the surface, and forms the grand men, who are the leaders and examples, rather than the companions of the race. . . . For that reality let us stand: that let us serve, and for that speak. Only as that shines through them, are these times or any times worth consideration." The lines have, from the beginning to end, a Transcendental ring. They are pointedly akin, too, here and there in tone to passages in the writings of Cousin and Jouffroy.

Another article in *The Dial* of October, 1842, entitled " The Conservative," breathes the essence of Transcendentalism. We cite from it the following telling lines: " There is always a certain meanness in the argument of conservatism, joined with a certain superiority in its fact. It affirms because it holds. . . . Conservatism makes no poetry, breathes no prayer, has no invention; it is all memory. . . . Reform in its antagonism inclines to asinine resistance, to kick with its hoofs; it runs to egotism and bloated self-conceit. . . . (But) the boldness of the hope men entertain transcends all former experience. It calms and cheers them with the picture of a simple and equal life of truth and piety."

[1] Cf. Cousin: "The language of inspiration is poetry." *Q. v.* page 35.
[2] Cf. Jouffroy: "Of all the great truths which have influenced the destinies of the human race, I know not one which originated in the instinct of the mass; they have all been the discoveries of gifted individuals, and the fruit of the solitary meditations of thinking men." *Q. v.* page 51.

In an article in the July, 1841, issue of *The Dial*, entitled "Prophecy — Transcendentalism — Progress," we have Transcendentalism from one point of view more or less bravely defined: " What is poetry, the poetic spirit, but the faculty of insight of the Good, the Beautiful, and the True, in the outward universe, and in the mysterious depths of the human spirit; that inward sense, which alone gives significance and relation to the objects of the material senses; by which man recognizes and believes in the Infinite and Absolute. . . . Transcendentalism is the recognition in man of the capacity of knowing truth intuitively, or of obtaining a scientific knowledge of an order of existence transcending the reach of the senses, and of which we can have no sensible experience. . . . Lumps of ice, or a lump of ice and flint may be rubbed together a good while, before a spark is struck; they will be lump of ice and flint still. . . . The senses, alone, can by no possibility arrive at the idea of cause, and are, therefore, impotent to furnish the first link in one of the chains of argument most relied on to demonstrate the reality of a First Cause. . . . Intuition is the only electric current that can evolve it. The idea of causation is a pure intellectual intuition." [1]

Divers passages excerpted here and there from articles in *The Dial* bear, it may readily be seen, a general resemblance to certain of the utterances of Cousin and Jouffroy. We quote at random: " The mind makes laws for itself, and changes those laws when it pleases so to do." [2]   " There is no soul which does not desire, think, and act; in other words, there is no soul without sensibility, intelligence, and power." [3]   " The most characteristic feature of modern thought is its subjectiveness." [4]

The French Eclectics now and then refer with evident familiarity to matter from Hindu and Pythagorean philosophy. We come across several columns in Margaret Fuller's periodical devoted wholly to quotations from these writings, viz., the " Laws of

---

[1] Cf. Cousin: "We do not commune with reflection, but with intuition," *q. v.* page 37.   Also Jouffroy: "Man believes by instinct and doubts by reason," *q. v.* page 52.

[2] *Q. v. The Dial*, January, 1842, article of W. B. G.

[3] *Q. v. Ibid.*

[4] *Q. v. The Dial*, April, 1844, anonymous article. Cf. Cousin on Fichte: "The one is no longer considered merely as the measure, but as the principal of all things."

Menu," [1] the " Veeshnu Sarma," [2] and " Pythagorean Sayings." [3] We find cited from the " Laws of Menu " the following somewhat noteworthy passages: " The soul is its own witness; the soul itself is its own refuge: offend not thy conscience soul, the supreme internal witness of men." " All that depends on another gives pain; all that depends upon himself gives pleasure; let him know this to be in a few words the definition of pleasure and pain." " Whatever is hard to be traversed, whatever is hard to be acquired, whatever is hard to be visited, whatever is hard to be performed, all this may be accomplished by true devotion; for the difficulty of devotion is the greatest of all." Two passages from the " Veeshnu Sarma " seem worthy of mention: " Fortune attendeth that lion amongst men who exerteth himself." " The mind of a good man does not alter when he is in distress; the waters of the ocean are not to be heated by a touch of straw." And, finally, as having in slight degree the ear-marks of Transcendentalism, we cite two or three passages from Jamblichus's " Life of Pythagoras," compiled by A. B. Alcott and published in the April, 1842, number of *The Dial:* " When the wise man opens his mouth, the beauties of his soul present themselves to view, like the statues of a temple." " It is not death but a bad life that destroys soul." "The soul is illumined by the recollection of divinity." [4]

As a votary and disseminator of Transcendentalism in New England Margaret Fuller — editor of *The Dial* — is, like her contemporaries, unique. To be *en rapport* with the Infinite and Eternal, to have no limits set for the development of her powers, — these seem to be Transcendental strings upon which she constantly harps. From the German and French philosophers of the later eighteenth and early nineteenth centuries, in particular from the poet Goethe, she derived the fixed notion that the fundamental duty of a human being is the duty of self-improvement. The sermonizing spirit is not conspicuous in her writings: she was not

[1] *Q. v. The Dial,* July, 1843, quotations from Sir Wm. Jones translation, in *The Dial.*
[2] *Q. v. Ibid,* quotations from Charles Wilkins's translation.
[3] *Q. v.* Selections by A. B. Alcott in *The Dial,* April, 1842.
[4] Cf. Jouffroy: "Whence come these deas which we find within us? From the divine mind, which is their natural home, and from which human reason is an emanation."

distinctly a moralist. But the personal note of an earnest and aspiring woman of letters is assuredly much in evidence.

The utterances of this unique feminine Transcendentalist indicate, however, indubitable evidences of acumen and breadth of outlook, — " Utopia it is impossible to build up. At least, mý hopes for our race on this planet are more limited than those of most of my friends. I accept the limitations of human nature, and believe a wise acknowledgment of them one of the best conditions of progress." It is interesting to compare the element of common sense in this passage with the common sense for which our French philosophers are proverbially noted. Margaret Fuller, too, was above the jealous vigilance which would abolish classes. Humanity, she avers, longs for upper strata of society, and is benefited by them. The unrighteousness of class distinctions consisted, in her mind, in making them out of clothes, trinkets, manners, instead of out of genuine culture. " Man tells us," she adds in her febrile way but with considerable compass of comprehension, " his aspiration in God; but in his demon he shows his depth of experience; and casts light into the cavern through which he worked his course up to the cheerful day."

Weak-mindedness was not in truth a trait of this Minerva with Transcendental tendencies in the realm of New-England letters. Her intellectuality was apparently inveterate. Her religious devotion, such as she had, consisted for the most part in strong admiration for the mystery of life and its manifestations. One of her most significant utterances, evincing at once clearness of vision, naïve frankness, and worthy idealism, is, it seems to us, the following, — " I am wanting in that intuitive tact and polish, which nature has bestowed upon some, but which I must acquire. And, on the other hand, my powers of intellect, although sufficient, I suppose, are not well disciplined. Yet all such hindrances may be overcome by an ardent spirit. If I fail, my consolation shall be found in active employment." For all of us it is hard to keep our heads cool. For a woman of Margaret Fuller's temperament and aspirations, philosophic equanimity and discretion were naturally doubly difficult. But she seems, nevertheless, to have attained in the course of her life and writings in no small measure to philosophical strength.

Our survey of some phases of *The Dial* and certain of the writings of this remarkable woman would scarcely be complete were we to omit giving attention to some of her characteristic oddities. " You walked into church," said Elizabeth Peabody to her, " as if you felt superior to everybody there." " Well, I did feel so," was the terse rejoinder. Her famous volume, " Women in the Nineteenth Century," is opened with the following quotations: "'Frailty, thy name is woman,' " and " ' The earth waits for her queen ' "; and the author continues: " The connection between these quotations may not be obvious, but it is strict. Yet would any contradict us, if we made them applicable to the other side, and began also: Frailty, thy name is Man. The Earth waits for its King." The touch, eminently feminine, strikes a contentious note which a greater mind would have avoided. The acute but delicate estimate which Emerson draws of her is significant: " In conversation Margaret seldom, except as a special grace, admitted others upon an equal ground with herself. She was exceedingly tender when she pleased to be, and most cherishing in her influence; but to elicit this tenderness, it was necessary to submit first to her personality. When a person was overwhelmed by her, and answered not a word, except, ' Margaret, be merciful to me, a sinner,' then her love and tenderness would come like a seraph's, and often an acknowledgment that she had been too harsh. . . . But her instinct was not humility, — that was always an afterthought."

We are told in the " Laws of Menu" that " At no age ought a woman to be allowed to govern herself as she pleases." This seems, in view of the modern woman suffrage movement, a rigorously conservative statement. But all through life Margaret Fuller stood forth almost too stanchly for her own and others' individualism and freedom. It is possible she might have been a wiser and happier woman, and her periodical, *The Dial*, had a wider and longer vogue, had she been somewhat less radically disposed.

3. Amos Bronson Alcott

Amos Bronson Alcott, noted for his " Orphic Sayings," does not manifest in any great degree the influence of the French Eclectics.

In a passage in his "Days from a Diary"[1] he definitely alludes somewhat disparagingly to "those French Eclectics." But this — so
far as one is able by a cursory survey to discover — is the only explicit reference in his writings to French philosophers of the early
nineteenth century.

Alcott, in fact, appears to be the only one of the New-England
Transcendentalists, whom we have under consideration, who was
impatient of the philosophy of the French Eclectics and antago-
nistic toward their disposition to temporize, compromise, mediate.
But this after all is not strange; for all through life Alcott was a
thorough-going idealist, an out-and-out extremist, not likely to
feel drawn toward a philosophy distinguished for moderation and
half-measures. Alcott, too, was primarily a talker, a conversa-
tionalist, an utterer of " oracles," rather than a deep student of
philosophy and letters; and although he may have had no con-
scious sympathy with Cousin, Jouffroy, or even Fourier, he indubit-
ably voices some of these philosophers' ideas which were in the
air in New England during his time. And, finally, his explicit
disparaging allusion to the writings of the French Eclectics indi-
cates, in itself, if not sympathy at least some measure of familiarity
with them.

As a contributor to *The Dial*, as the founder of the *Fruitlands*
community, and as a *reformer* with the most sanguine Transcendental tendencies, Alcott stands enrolled as one of the chief figures
of the Transcendental Movement in New England. Emerson, in
a letter from Concord to an English friend, thus aptly characterizes
our New-England oracle: " About this time, or perhaps a few
weeks later, we shall send you a large piece of spiritual New
England in the shape of A. Bronson Alcott, who is to sail for London
about the 20th of April, and whom you must not fail to see, if you
can compass it. A man who cannot write, but whose conversation
is unrivalled in its way; such insight, such discernment of spirit,
such pure intellectual play, such revolutionary impulses of thought.
Whilst he speaks he has no peer, and yet, all men say, ' such partiality of view.' I, who hear the same charge always laid at my
own gate, do not so readily feel that fault in my friend. But I en-

---

[1] Days from a Diary, A. B. Alcott. See *The Dial*, April, 1842.

treat you to see this man. Since Plato and Plotinus we have not had his like." [1]

This " large piece of spiritual New England," this self-appointed " oracle " of his time, was born at Wolcott, Connecticut, November 20, 1799. He was of humble extraction, the son of a farmer, and his first experience of life was gained as a pedler in the South.

About 1828 he became an educational reorganizer and established in Boston a school [2] which attracted much attention. His teaching was largely conversational; specimens of his socratic pedagogical talks are to be found in his "Conversation with Children on the Gospel," which appeared in 1836. Some of the ornaments which adorned the walls of his unique school in Masonic Temple, Boston, were: a head of Jesus, a bust of Plato, bust of Socrates, bust of Milton, and a picture of Dr. Channing. Emerson wrote in his *Journal* concerning the reform educator: " Alcott declares that a teacher is one who can assist the child in obeying his own mind, and who can remove all unfavorable circumstances. . . . He measures ages by leaders, and reckons history by Pythagoras, Plato, Jesus." But Alcott's methods, although commendably lofty, proved to be too impractical; his school fell out of favor; and so, abandoning it, he removed to Concord.

During his stay at Concord, the storm-center of New-England Transcendentalism, he disseminated all sorts of Utopian views on theology, education, society, vegetarianism, and what not. He gave now and then lectures which won quite widespread attention by virtue of their benignity and originality.

In 1842, however, our visionary departed for England. Returning a few months later with some English friends he endeavored to found a kind of phalanstery, called *Fruitlands*, near the village of Harvard in Massachusetts. The farm, located between Worcester and Nashua, some thirty miles from Boston, lay on a hillside gently sloping toward the Nashua River; it was a remote place, without a road, surrounded by a beautiful landscape of New-England woods and fields, an ideal sylvan spot for the realization of Utopian views. But the family, which never numbered more

---

[1] From a letter of Emerson to Stirling, Concord, April 1, 1842.

[2] Cf. Record of a School, by Elizabeth Palmer Peabody, J. Munroe & Co. Boston, 1835.

than twelve, did not hold together more than six months. The experiment, like the other Transcendental company — the Brook Farm Society, was an outgrowth of the psychical upheaval of the time, and especially of the French philosopher Fourier's ideal of co-operation in phalansteries. The spirit which animated the little colony is aptly set forth in the following passage from an article in *The Dial* of April, 1843: " The inner nature of every member of the Family is at no time neglected. A constant leaning on the living spirit within the soul should consecrate every talent to holy uses, cherishing the widest charities. The choice Library [1] is accessible to all who are desirous of perusing these records of piety and wisdom. . . . Pledged to the spirit [2] alone, the founders can anticipate no hasty or numerous accession to their numbers. . . ."

In addition to his distinction as master of a Pestalozzian school and founder of a Fourierian phalanstery, Alcott is noteworthy for his contributions to *The Dial*. In his articles for this organ we find set forth the acme of New-England idealism; but it is idealism divorced from common sense and without the saving grace of humor. The series of papers under the title of "Days from a Diary," magniloquent in tone, unsystematic in thought, highfalutin in sentiment, constitute the most memorable of his *Dial* effusions.

We might give as Alcott's favorite authors, Plato, Pythagoras, and Swedenborg; and the names of the first two one comes across frequently in the pages of Cousin and Jouffroy. Emerson, of course, was Alcott's criterion among New-England colleagues. The way, indeed, in which he blends Emersonian optimism and idealism is particularly characteristic. We quote a significant passage apropos of aspiration: " She (aspiration) would breathe life, organize light; her hope is eternal; a never-ending, still-beginning quest of the Godhead in her own bosom." It is interesting to compare with this passage some analogous lines from Cousin: " Inspiration is accompanied with that forcible emotion, which bears the soul away from its ordinary and subaltern state and disengages from it the sublime and godlike portion of its nature." [3]

---

[1] Cf. *The Dial*, April, 1843, Catalogue of Books.
[2] Cf. Social Tendency, *The Dial*, July, 1843.
[3] *Q. v.* Cousin, page 35.

For his sermonizing spirit this somewhat elementary yet quite well-meaning philosopher of Concord is as remarkable as for anything. When he begins to preach he forthwith appears, as if by some occult right, in his natural element. The following specimens of his proficiency along the sermonizing line are superb enough to make the ordinary mind at least temporarily start and stare: "Step by step one climbs the pinnacles of existence; life itself is but the stretch for that mountain of holiness. Opening here with humanity, 'tis the aiming at divinity in ever-ascending circles of aspiring and endeavor. Who ceases to aspire dies. Our pursuits are our prayers, our ideals our gods." [1]

Alcott, in short, appears to have been an innocent attitudinizer and moralizer. Without accurate scholarship or profound learning, he yet honestly endeavored, in his own high and simple way, to lead a life of self-culture and self-development. Emerson somewhat unaccountably pronounced him a most extraordinary man, the highest genius of his time; and beyond doubt he was a pure and upright personality, of an idealistic Transcendental bent, who lived a more or less serene and benevolent life.

His prime defect obviously lies in the fact that he did not possess a sufficiently large bump of sanity. A little more study at first hand of the writings of the very French Eclectics whom he disparages, and sympathy with their clear and level-headed common sense, might have saved him from being, as he at times was, the butt of merriment. Such statements as these betray him, —

> "Identity halts in diversity."
> "The poles of things are integrated."
> "Love globes, wisdom orbs, all things."
> "Always are the divine Gemini intertwined."

4. Ralph Waldo Emerson

As time passes Emerson's utterances in the field of American literature, unlike those of his fellow Transcendentalists, tend to take higher and more enduring place. He was the finest flower

[1] Days from a Diary, April, 1842.

of at least six generations of refined culture and pious living, a profound and independent lover of truth and beauty in philosophy and literature, the personal friend of such idealists as Wordsworth and Carlyle. He was, in short, a kind of felicitous blend of the Hebrew, the Greek, and the Yankee. He was not merely "the Poet and Seer" of the Transcendental Movement in New England of his time, he has become as well no small figure in world literature. The Bible and Shakspere, Plato and Swedenborg, were his paragons. He was, withal, undoubtedly acquainted with the writings of the French Eclectics, and was one of the chief factors in effecting the efflorescence of Idealism, or Transcendentalism, here in America.

We find several instances of Emerson's familiarity with the writings of the French philosophers with whom we are especially concerned. He was, in the first place, one of the assistant editors of *The Dial* — the chief organ of New-England Transcendentalism — for two years, from 1840 to 1842, and was editor-in-chief of the paper, after the resignation of Margaret Fuller, from 1842 to 1844. During his office as editor of *The Dial* there appeared on the pages of this periodical various references to the writings of French philosophers,[1] — three concerning Cousin, two concerning Jouffroy, and at least one concerning Fourier. In addition to these instances from *The Dial* of Emerson's acquaintance with the writings of French philosophers, we come across in his essays in the Complete Works edition, published by Houghton, Mifflin and Company, several passages in the course of which — along with cursory references to such writings as those of the Veddas, and the Laws of Menu, of Heraclitus, Plato, Pythagoras, Plotinus, Marcus Aurelius, Swedenborg, Böhme, Kant, Fichte, Hegel, Berkeley, Cudworth, Wordsworth, Coleridge, Carlyle, and others — he makes several definite allusions to Cousin, Fourier, and others.

Insomuch as these definite allusions to French philosophers have direct bearing on the subject at hand, we cite at random a few of them. In the essay entitled "Intellect" in the Essays, First Series, we find Emerson writing as follows: "A new doctrine seems at first a subversion of all our opinions, tastes, and manner of living. Such has Swedenborg, such has Kant, such has Coleridge, such

---

[1] *Q. v.* pages 70 and 71 in Chapter on Margaret Fuller.

has Hegel or his interpreter Cousin seemed to many young men in this County." [1]   Again in the biographical sketch of his aunt, " Mary Moody Emerson," Emerson refers explicitly to Cousin in the following passage: " Her early reading was Milton, Young Akenside, Samuel Clarke, Jonathan Edwards, and always the Bible. Later, Plato, Plotinus, Marcus Antoninus, Stewart, Coleridge, Cousin, Herder, Locke, Madame De Staël," [2] . . . We happen here and there in the course of Emerson's writings upon manifold references to Fourier; the citation of two of these ought to be sufficient. In " Life and Letters in New England," we note this passage: " Fourier, almost as wonderful an example of the mathematical mind of France as La Place or Napoleon, turned a truly vast arithmetic to the question of social misery." [3] And in " The Man of Letters " Emerson writes in a somewhat less complimentary strain: " A French prophet of our age, Fourier, predicated that one day, instead of by battles and Ecumenical Councils, the rival portions of humanity would dispute each other's excellence in the manufacture of little cakes." [4]   Emerson naturally enough, makes now and then allusions to various French writers such as Madame De Staël, Benjamin Constant, Guizot, and others, also to the French spirit in literature and social life; but with these indefinite allusions hinting of French influence we are not particularly concerned. Let us proceed, then, to a critical appreciation of Emerson's writings themselves, and the element of the Transcendental in them.

" Look into thy heart, and write," is the counsel of Sir Philip Sidney; and Emerson seems happily to have followed this counsel all through his career of letters. He had, moreover, a pure and noble soul; and when he looked into it, and wrote out of it, he said pure and noble things. His now more or less immortal essays are fairly crammed with thoughts of a rare order. There are so many, indeed, and they are of such variety, that it is difficult to determine

---

[1] Q. v. Intellect, Essays, First Series, page 320, H., M. & Co., Boston, 1895.

[2] Q. v. Mary Moody Emerson, Litarary and Biographical Sketches, page 376, H., M. & Co., Boston, 1895.

[3] Q. v. Life and Letters in New England, L. and B. S., page 327, H., M. & Co., Boston, 1895.

[4] Q. v. The Man of Letters, L. and B. S., page 235, H., M. & Co., Boston, 1895.

on those which are most significant. Like all great writers his genius goes, in its own way, almost the whole range of human thought and feeling. Like a true Transcendentalist that he is, too, his works bear unmistakable ear-marks of certain traits of Transcendentalism as indicated in the writings of his fellow New-England Transcendentalists and the contemporary French Eclectics; they evince here and there, and often simultaneously, — optimistic note, breadth of outlook, faith in an inner light, self-reliance, idealism, and sanity.

The optimistic note, in the utterance of Emerson, is apparently not only natural but irrepressible. Sincerely and instinctively he bursts forth, as do at times in a similar spirit both Cousin and Jouffroy, into such expressions as, — " What is excellent, as God lives is permanent." " There is no object so foul that intense light will not make it beautiful." " A divine person is the prophecy of the mind; a friend is the hope of the heart." " All great men find eternity affirmed in the very promise of their faculties." " God is the All-fair: Truth and Goodness and Beauty are but different faces of the same All." And as a final instance of his optimistic spirit we cannot omit citing the following lines from his stanza apropos of *character:*

> "The sun set; but set not his hope;
> Stars rose; his faith was earlier up:
> Fixed on the enormous galaxy,
> Deeper and older seemed his eye:
> And matched his sufferance sublime
> The taciturnity of time."

Although at times from particular viewpoints Emerson's thoughts may appear contradictory, they nevertheless possess as a whole unusual breadth, vitality, and integrity. Neither Cousin nor his disciple Jouffroy, standing for cosmopolitan eclecticism as they do, are more liberal or universal in compass of thought and feeling than Emerson. The following lines illustrate in a somewhat rich and poetic vein his breadth of outlook: " Poetry was all written before time was, and whenever we are so finely organized that we can penetrate into that region where the air is music, we can hear those primal warblings and attempt to write them down." [1] It is interesting and informing to compare with this passage those significant lines from Cousin: "The language of inspiration is poetry."

Faith in an inner light goes hand in hand, in the make-up of this true Transcendentalist, with breadth of outlook. By faith in an inner light we are to understand simply faith in our own spontaneous impulses, or revelations, as evidences of the Infinite and Eternal Life welling up in us and circulating through us. As Emerson, himself, puts it: "Like a bird which alights nowhere, but hops perpetually from bough to bough, is the Power which abides in no man and in no woman, but for a moment speaks from this one, and for another moment from that one." [2] Further evidences of Emerson's faith in an inner light are to be found in such passages as: "Our spontaneous action is always best." "We love characters in proportion as they are impulsive and spontaenous." [3] "It (character) is conceived of as a certain undemonstrable force, a Familiar or Genius, by whose impulses the man is guided but whose counsels he cannot impart." [4] And, finally, — "Out of yourself should come your theme, and only thus can your genius be your friend."

Emerson, moreover, cannot be dissociated from such lines as, — "Trust thyself; every heart vibrates to that iron string." But self-reliance in the sage of Concord is no silly vanity, no fatuous wilfulness; it is just the natural and inevitable result of the man's greatness of heart and mind. His invariable self-reliance appears to spring, indeed, from a certain innate power and poise, from a certain native sweetness, soundness, and sanity of character. He was self-reliant because he could not be otherwise; and he was the outspoken advocate of it because he clearly realized that, kept within the bounds of moderation and social good sense, it is the only avenue open to all of us for the attainment on earth of happi-

---

[1] Q. v. The Poet.

[2] Q. v. Experience.

[3] Cf. Cousin: "Spontaneity is the genius of humanity, as philosophy is the genius of some men."

[4] With this cf. Jouffroy, page 51: "(Our sense of duty arises) from a certain number of truths a priori, which, in making their appearance in our understanding, illuminate the creation with a searchlight, reveal the meaning of it, solve the problem and unfold its law."

ness. We cite a few passages, noteworthy for the spirit of self-reliance, which constitute a kind of keynote to his character and utterance: " Nothing can bring you peace but yourself." [1] " What your heart thinks great, is great: the soul's emphasis is always right." " Character is ·centrality, the impossibility of being displaced or overset." " We believe in ourselves as we do not believe in others." " The great man is he who in the midst of the crowd keeps with perfect sweetness the independence of solitude." " Discontent is want of self-reliance: it is infirmity of will." " Valor consists in the power of self-recovery, so that a man cannot have his flank turned, cannot be outgeneraled, but put him where you will, he stands." " Self-trust is the essence of heroism." And, as if to himself, he writes, — " Doubt not, O poet, but persist: Say 't is in me, and shall out! " [2]

Ever living in an atmosphere of hope and confidence, of courage and charity, it is no wonder that Emerson is idealistic. His whole nature, pure and noble to the core, provided just the soil on which idealism is wont to flourish. Admiration and love inevitably follow in the wake of the idealistic concepts which he launches forth; he tinges all that he saw with the rosy hue of his own soul. We quote the following two noteworthy passages as illustrative of his idealism: " Hitch your wagon to a star. Let us not fag in paltry works which serve our pot and bag alone. Let us not lie and steal. No God will help. We shall find all their teams going the other way, — Charles' Wain, Great Bear, Orion, Leo, Hercules: every God will leave us. Work rather for those interests which the divinities honor and promote, — justice, love, freedom, knowledge, utility." [3] " Poets are liberating gods. . . . Those who are free throughout the world. . . . I think nothing is of value in books excepting the transcendental and extraordinary." [4]

[1] Cf. Hindu Literature, Laws of Menu: "All that depends on another gives pain; all that depends on himself gives pleasure; let him know this to be in few words the definition of pain and pleasure." Also cf. Milton, Paradise Lost: "The mind in its own place and in itself can make a heaven of hell, a hell of heaven."
[2] Cf. Cousin, page 37: "Every man, if he knows himself, knows all the rest, nature and God at the same time with himself."
[3] Q. v. Civilization.
[4] Q. v. The Poet. Cf. also Jouffroy: " Whence come these (religious) ideas which we find within us? From the divine mind, which is their natural and eternal home, and from which human reason is an emanation."

It might shock our sense of the equilibrium of things to find that Emerson with all his patent merits should have no shortcomings. His temper of mind for a human being is a bit too cool and lofty. His feeling for shades and shadows in thought and sentiment is somewhat deficient. In dramatic power, too, in the sense for the pathetic and tragic in life, he has many peers. The defect of lack of common sense, of every-day sanity, however, assuredly cannot be laid at his door. Now and then in a passage he may startle us with some sublimated extravagance; but, shortly, a line or so of sterling good sense clears the mist of unreality away. At times, indeed, one is puzzled to tell which ranks uppermost in Emerson's writings — as in those of Cousin and Jouffroy — literary genius or practical good sense. We quote several passages which speak for themselves:

"In a good lord there must first be a good animal."

"Good manners are made up of petty sacrifices."

"The gentleman is a man of truth, lord of his own actions, and express-ing that lordship in his behavior; . . . the word denotes good-nature or benevolence; manhood first, and then gentleness."

"A flint and a genius that will not strike fire are no better than wet junkwood."

"A man is a golden impossibility. The line he must walk is a hair's breadth. The wise through excess of wisdom is made a fool."

"The terror of cloudless noon, the emerald of Polycrates, the awe of prosperity, the instinct which leads every generous soul to impose on itself tasks of noble asceticism and vicarious virtue, are the tremblings of the balance of justice through the heart and mind of man."

"Human life is made up of two elements, power and form, and the proportion must be invariably kept if we would have it sweet and sound."

Emerson, it is true, has not the systematic, constructive genius of a Plato, a Kant, or even of his contemporary French philosophers, — Cousin and Jouffroy; but he has, nevertheless, a certain nobility of thought and utterance, decidedly Transcendental in tone, which gains our admiration. He impresses us as being an endless seeker after more life and light without any past at his back. As a French critic, M. René de Poyen Belleisle, puts it, — "il est encore quelque chose de plus pour nous, et nous pouvons, certes, lui appliquer la definition du philosophe que Thoreau [1] a faite : ' To be a philosopher is not merely to have subtle thoughts, or even to found a school, but so to love wisdom as to live according to its dictates a life of independence, simplicity, magnanimity, and trust.' "

5. Brook Farm (Fourier)

In the July, 1842, number of *The Dial* there is an anonymous article appertaining to Fourier. It calls attention to the increasing zeal and numbers of the disciples of Fourier in America and Europe, and acknowledges that their theories and projects are worthy of respectful attention. The article, too, remarks with some surprise on certain coincidences between the French Socialist Fourier and the Swedish Transcendentalist, Swedenborg. " Fourier," the writer informs us, " has skipped no fact but one, namely, Life. He treats man as a plastic thing, something that may be put up or down, ripened or retarded, moulded, polished, made into solid, or fluid, or gas, at the will of the leader.". The writer, however, concludes his article in a more favorable vein with the following comment: " Yet in a day of small, sour, and fierce schemes, one is admonished and cheered by a project (Fourier's scheme of Socialism) of such friendly aims, and of such bold and generous proportion." The social condition of mankind, according to the author of another article [2] in the same number of *The Dial*, needs to be vastly improved. A great genius, we are told, must arise, piercing the veil that shrouds in mystery the universe, and revealing to us the laws of order and harmony which govern creation. And that genius, says this second contributor to *The Dial*, has arisen and appeared before us in the form of the French Socialist and Idealist, — Fourier.

These two articles in *The Dial* hint of the vogue of Fourier amongst the Transcendentalists of New England, and the esteem in which he and his idealistic schemes were in some instances

---

[1] Henry David Thoreau (1817–1862), the noteworthy poet-naturalist of New England, contemporary and disciple of Emerson.
[2] Means of Effecting a Final Reconciliation between Religion and Science, *The Dial*, July, 1842.

held. But Fourier's influence in America ripened into more concrete fruit than mere critical review articles in *The Dial;* under the influence of his philosophy several socialistic communities were founded here in the States, — among which were the *Brook Farm,* the *Fruitlands,* the *Hopedale,* the *Northampton,* and the *New Harmony* communities. Of all these various socialistic communities the most successful, and for our purposes the most significant, was the *Brook Farm* community of West Roxbury, Massachusetts.

The West Roxbury Association, or *The Brook Farm Community,* was organized by a select number of New-England men and women of Transcendental tendencies. They wished to form an ideal society — based on the Fourier scheme of phalansteries — on Puritan ground; they bought for the purpose a farm in West Roxbury, Massachusetts, of about two hundred acres; and took possession of the place sometime in April, 1841. George Ripley was elected president of the association; Charles Dana (later editor of *The New York Tribune*) was elected secretary; and William Allen acted as head farmer. Some members took shares in the community by paying money; others by giving labor. Work was distributed, in accordance with the theories of Fourier, by committees; there were for members such various employments as shoemaking, dressmaking, farming, cooking, teaching. Some notable men and women, attracted by the beauty of location and the culture of the members, became boarders at the institution. George William Curtis of New York and his brother from Oxford, England, were charter members of the society. Theodore Parker, Ralph Waldo Emerson, Margaret Fuller, and Nathaniel Hawthorne were frequent visitors. Margaret Fuller, by virtue of her genius in conversation and abundant sympathy, was one of the most frequent and welcome of the guests. Hawthorne's gentle yet aloof Puritanical genius fails, one cannot help thinking, to do justice both to the community itself, and to Margaret Fuller's relation with it, in his novel apropos of the society, entitled " The Blithedale Romance." [1]

Emerson in characterizing the *Brook Farm* organization says: " It was a noble and generous movement in the projectors, to try

[1] Cf. Blithedale Romance, Nathaniel Hawthorne, H., M. & Co.

an experiment of better living. They had the feeling that our ways of living were too conventional and expensive, not allowing each to do what he had a talent for, and not permitting men to combine cultivation of mind and heart with a reasonable amount of daily labor. At the same time, it was an attempt to lift others with themselves, and to share the advantages they should attain, with others now deprived of them." [1]

And Elizabeth Palmer Peabody, another contemporary of the movement, in an article in the January, 1842, number of *The Dial*, describes and criticises in the following words the Fourier experiment at West Roxbury: " A few individuals reacting from social evils . . . have determined to become the Faculty of an Embryo University. . . . They have bought a farm, in order to make agriculture the basis of their life, it being the most direct and simple in relation to nature. . . . The plan of the community, as an Economy, is for all who have property to take stock and receive a fixed interest thereon. . . . All labor, whether bodily or intellectual, is to be paid at the same rate of wages; on the principle, that as the labor becomes merely bodily, it is a greater sacrifice to the individual laborer, to give his time to it; because his time is desirable for the cultivation of the intellect, in exact proportion to ignorance. . . . Some say, . . . they (the *Brook Farm* people) are doubtless transcendentalists. But to mass a few protestants together and call them transcendentalists is popular cant. Transcendentalism belongs to no sect of religion, and no social party." [2]

The society, like other idealistic communities attempted on a socialistic basis since the beginning of time, shortly after its organization began to disintegrate. The " Perpetual Picnic," the " Eldorado of New England," the " Age of Reason in a Patty-pan," evinced even in its initial stages certain fatal weaknesses. The institution became a sort of whispering gallery; the life in common was found to be too brassy and too boarding-house-like. The mothers finding in addition to other discomforts that the phalanstery nursery — against human nature and good sense — deprived them of their children, gradually decided against the community. The strain on courtesy and good humor became, in general, too

---

[1] Cf. Life and Letters in New England.
[2] *The Dial*, January, 1842, article by E. P. P.

hard to bear; the irksome work that had to be done, such as planting by the men, and washing by the women, was quite often selfishly shirked; the community had no authorized head except the president, George Ripley, who was inclined to be too rigorous in his theoretical ideals; and each member being for the most part his own master and mistress, things sooner or later began to go at sixes and sevens. The bonds of common sympathy and interest became loosened; members here and there on this or that pretext dribbled away; and, finally, with the accidental burning to the ground of one of the chief buildings, the whole association went to pieces.

When the *Brook Farm Association* broke up many sustained heavy pecuniary loss. And the whole affair from a financial point of view was a flat failure. But the idealistic socialistic experiment, on the French philosopher Fourier's plan, was not without some measure of success: a more intimate knowledge of human nature and the ways of the world was gained; the close association of members resulted in a general uplifting of the standard of culture; and the outcome of each seeing the other's strength and weakness at close range was in the end a more charitable mutual understanding, and a more genuine mutual respect. The whole movement was simply a natural, almost inevitable, symptom of the time, the place, and the people. It was, in a small way, an essential step in the development of Transcendentalism in New England.

Fourierism, the theories and principles upon which the *Brook Farm* experiment was based, appears, moreover, to be, characteristically French. The English socialistic tendencies, such as those of Robert Owen,[1] have a distinctly material basis; and although sentiment of a religious or sympathetic sort may be appended, it is usually added only as tasteful ornament. French social tendencies, however, such as those of Saint-Simon and his successor Fourier, tend to combine the material and the spiritual; they compass and incorporate from the beginning manifold questions touching the feelings, sympathies, and ideals of human nature. It is quite patent, then, why the Fourier scheme of socialism appealed more to the Transcendentalists of New England than the Robert Owen or any other scheme of community life.

The analogy between the socialism of the idealist Fourier and

---

[1] Robert Owen of Lanark came to New England about 1845.

the mysticism of the idealist Swedenborg, both of which appealed strongly to the Transcendentalists of New England, is interesting. The general view upon which Fourier proceeds is this: there is in the Divine Mind a certain social order, to which man is destined, and which is discoverable by man. There are, according to Fourier, twelve fundamental passions in man, consisting, firstly, of the five senses; and secondly, of the four social passions, — friendship, ambition, love, and the parental sentiment; and thirdly, of three intellectual powers, — Cabalism, Alternation, and Emulation, whatever these three may be. Swedenborg, in a somewhat similar sublimated strain, declares that man's soul is made up of Loves, and every Love must find its Wisdom. Fourier would have the Love (Feminine) and Wisdom (Masculine) in human nature, as set forth by Swedenborg, or the twelve passions, as formulated by himself, find their proper development by the law of groups and series. If they do not, he argues, they become principles of disorder, and engender the world of wickedness and disorder that we see around us.

The *Brook Farm* experiment, we understand, was instituted by certain New-England Transcendentalists in order to try to realize in tangible form the abstract ideals of two of their favorite European philosophers, — the French Socialist, Charles Fourier, and the Swedish Mystic, Emanuel Swedenborg. That the New-England idealists in due time found their American minds too fond of plain dealing to prosper under the somewhat eccentric régimes formulated by certain of their European preceptors, is not remarkable. The important issues of the experiment for us are that it was projected by New-England Transcendentalists under the spell of a notable French idealist's influence, that it was instrumental in gathering together for several years into a cogent unit on Massachusetts soil a large number of New-England Transcendentalists, notable masters in art, music, and letters,[1] and that its failure as an

[1] Among the notable Minor Transcendentalists who were associated with *The Brook Farm Community* of West Roxbury, and who have not already in this dissertation been explicitly mentioned in connexion with the experiment, are:

J. S. Dwight, of Boston, Massachusetts, the musical editor of the Brook Farm periodical, entitled *The Harbinger*.

J. F. Clarke, Unitarian minister of The Church of the Disciples, Boston, and author of various writings Transcendental in tone.

W. H. Channing, graduate of Harvard, the pastor of a Unitarian Church of

institution was effective in a most opportune way in establishing culture and wisdom in New England once and for all time on a broader and firmer basis.

Boston, the joint-editor of *The Harbinger*, and a frequent contributor to *The Dial.*

C. P. Cranch, graduate of the Divinity School at Cambridge, then a Unitarian clergyman, and finally a landscape painter and author.

Jones Very, of Salem, Massachusetts, graduated from Harvard, traveled abroad, was the personal friend of Clarke, Channing, and others, and became a poet of almost highfalutin tendencies.

C. A. Bartol, of Freeport, Maine, a graduate of Bowdoin College, and the Cambridge Divinity School; became pastor of West Church, Boston, and was early a member of the Transcendental Club.

IV. CONCLUSION

General Significance of French Influence on New-England Transcendentalism

THE office of bringing to a close this thesis on " French Philosophers and New-England Transcendentalism " now faces us. In Part I, an attempt was made to define Transcendentalism, to sketch miscellaneous precursors of the movement, and to trace the beginnings of the philosophy in New England. In Part II, French expositors of the movement were taken up, the way in which the movement was in part transmitted into France was pointed out, Victor Cousin's and Théodore Jouffroy's exposition of the philosophy set forth, and a few words in general were added concerning the aspect of Transcendentalism in French dress. In Part III, the New-England phase of the phenomena was dealt with, especially George Ripley's, Margaret Fuller's, A. Bronson Alcott's, and R. W. Emerson's affirmation of Transcendentalism, and the relation which obviously exists in greater or less degree between what the New-England Transcendentalists thought and said and what was uttered by French exponents of the movement. And now, finally, in Part IV, it is in order for us to round off the dissertation by drawing up some general conclusions concerning the significance of French influence, such as it is, in its relation to the New-England movement.

The similarity of the precursors of both the New-England Transcendentalists and the French philosophers is one of the facts which at once makes impression. Both the New-England Transcendentalists and the French philosophers, whom we have under consideration, frequently refer, as has been cursorily evinced, to such figures in the history of philosophy as the writers of the Vedas, as Plato, Pythagoras, Plotinus; as Fichte, Kant, and Hegel. Elements of idealism, more or less Transcendental in nature, appear, indeed, to have flourished widespread and intermingled throughout ancient and modern philosophy; and New-England Transcendentalists derived impetus quite apparently not only from the writings of French philosophers, but as well from the same sources in ancient and modern philosophy as the French philosophers turned to for inspiration.

French influence on New-England Transcendentalism was, then, it is evident, one among various more or less similar and correlated philosophical influences. In considering them, however, we find that the influence of French philosophy was not particularly predominant. In comparing the number of times that such representative New-England Transcendentalists as George Ripley, Amos Bronson Alcott, and Ralph Waldo Emerson refer to such miscellaneous philosophers as Menu, Heraclitus, Socrates, Plato, Zeno, Pythagoras, Plotinus, Jamblichus, Boehme, Swedenborg, Berkeley, Goethe, Fichte, Hegel, Schelling, Wordsworth, Coleridge, and others, with the number of times they refer to the French philosophers, Cousin, Jouffrey, and the socialist Fourier, we find that the number of times the French philosophers are mentioned appears in truth small. In the sixteen volumes of *The Dial*,[1] for instance, the chief organ of New-England Transcendentalism, the French philosophers Cousin, Jouffroy, and Fourier are referred to only about fifteen times; whereas Plato, the Greek philosopher, is mentioned over thirty times, and Fichte, the German idealist, is mentioned over twenty. In the " Specimens of Foreign Standard Literature," too, the editor, George Ripley, informs us in the Preface that " among the writers whom it is proposed to give translations are Cousin, Jouffroy, Guizot, and Benjamin Constant in French; and Herder, Schiller, Goethe, Wieland, Lessing, Jacobi, Fichte, Schelling, Richte, Novalis, Uhland, Korner, Voltz, Mentzel, Neander, Schleiermacher, De Wette, Olshausen, Ammon, Hase, and Twesen, in German." [2] Thus we see that the amount of attention devoted to French influence, Transcendental in nature, in the "Specimens of Foreign Standard Literature" as well as in *The Dial*, is, in proportion even to German influence alone, slight.

[1] Published quarterly, 1840–1844.
[2] *Q. v.* Edition of 1838.

Somewhat disappointing, we must acknowledge, seems the
slenderness of French influence.   The eclectic philosophers Cousin
and Jouffroy being in a measure the successors in France of the
German Transcendentalists, their idealistic philosophy of the
Restoration Period being admirably inclusive and pointed, and
the French language itself in which they wrote being somewhat
easier to comprehend by English speaking people than the German, one might naturally infer at first blush by exercising deduc-
tive reasoning that French influence in the early nineteenth century on New-England Transcendentalism would be not less, but
greater, than the German influence.   The case, however, turns
out to be quite otherwise.   The greater surge, boldness, originality
of the German idealists apparently appealed more strongly to the
young idealistic philosophers of New England than did the more
rational, urbane, compromise philosophy of the French Eclectics.
Nobly valorous, wittily discursive, sanely sociable as they are, the
French Eclectics, nevertheless, strike one as being more notable
for manners and convention, for graces and accomplishments,
for sophistication and cosmopolitanism than for anything highly
flavored of the Transcendental; yet the highly flavored Transcendental, such as is characteristic of the philosophy of the German
idealists of the later eighteenth and early nineteenth centuries,
was just what the New-England idealists of the early nineteenth
century experienced especial affinity for.   The French philosophers, Cousin, Jouffroy, and the socialist Fourier, we have found,
nevertheless, were well known to the Transcendentalists of New
England; their writings were widely read in the original and in
translation; and their influence on the New-England Transcendentalists, although not especially profound or extensive, is yet
distinctly appreciable.

The wide learning of the French philosophers, Cousin and
Jouffroy, exerted, we must believe, considerable influence.   The
French Eclectics helped, in other words, to extend the intellectual
horizon of the New-England Transcendentalists, were efficacious
in familiarizing them with the names of world-great philosophers,
and in acquainting them with the gist of world-great philosophical systems.   Cousin's comprehensive eclectic exposition of the
history of philosophy and Jouffroy's summary eclectic exposition

of the history of ethics — both of which, we have seen, were familiar through various editions in the original and in translation to the New-England Transcendentalists — are nothing short of masterly. " La philosophie," writes Cousin in his telling way, " dans tous les temps, roule sur les idées fondamentales du vrai, du beau, et du bien. L'idée du vrai, philosophiquement développée c'est la psychologie, la logique, la métaphysique; l'idée du bien, c'est la morale privée et publique; l'idée du beau, c'est cette science qu'en Allemagne on appelle l'esthétique, dont les détails regardent la critique littéraire et la critique des arts, mais dont les principes généraux ont toujours occupé une place plus ou moins considérable dans les recherches et même dans l'enseignement des philosophes, depuis Platon et Aristote jusqu'à Hutcheson et Kant." [1]

The rationality and urbanity for which the French are illustrious, too, must have been, in some measure at least, communicated to the New-England Transcendentalists and been more or less appreciably influential among them. The reputation of French men of letters in general and of the French Eclectics of the nineteenth century in particular for rationality and urbanity is generally recognized. *Comme il faut* is the watchword of the French. To make no noise, to be serene, to avoid the crass and the brusque, to be adaptable to society and externals, are their characteristics. French genius, in short, strives to achieve finished form, gracious manners, polished periods; it tends to manifest in the realm of literature and philosophy the fruit and flowers of the thoughts and feelings of the human race rather than the more basic grain or trunk. The men-of-letters spirit incarnated by George Ripley, Margaret Fuller, and Ralph Waldo Emerson was, we confidently aver, attributable in no small measure to the influence of the nineteenth century philosophers of the race of Madame de Staël, with whose writings these three New-Englanders were so patently familiar. It is interesting to note in this connection, as we have already pointed out, that A. Bronson Alcott, the only one among the New-England Transcendentalists guilty in his utterances of a Carlylean Germanic excess, is the very one

---

[1] Le Vrai, le Beau, le Bien — Discourse d'ouverture, 1827. Cf. book review notes in *The Dial*, October, 1842.

among the New-England Transcendentalists least acquainted with
the writings of the French Eclectics, and the only one who makes
disparaging reference to them.

The American mind and the French genius, one might say, fur-
thermore, present in common on the whole the characteristic of
common sense, " like that which Rose Flammock the weaver's
daughter in Scott's romance commends in her father, as resem-
bling a yardstick, which, whilst it measures dowlas and diaper,
can equally measure tapestry and cloth of gold." [1] But the American idealists of New England of the early nineteenth century
certainly needed example and instruction in amenity and moderation. And in the writings of the French Eclectics of the Restoration Period the right sort of tutorage was found; for the New-
England temper of the early nineteenth century inclining over-
much to such extremest views as the occultism of Plotinus, the
spiritualism of Swedenborg, and the ardent idealism of Fichte
was happily counterbalanced and equalized, in large measure,
by contact with the accurate and systematic mind, the spirit of
compromise and opportunism of the urbane French philosophers
of the Restoration Period. The philosophy of the New-England
Transcendentalists, in brief, was in a considerable degree rational-
ized and humanized by the instruction accorded by the French
Eclectics.

The element of idealism conspicuous both in the philosophy of
the French Eclectics and in the philosophy of the New-England
Transcendentalists is, too, in itself in a way significant. It helps
to show that there was in Europe in the nineteenth century a wave
of idealism in the air; it goes to prove that French philosophers
were active participants of this general idealistic movement abroad
in Germany, England, and America; and it incites us to discern,
as it were, processes of transmutation and development, however
obscure, in the idealistic or Transcendental movement in the
realm of philosophy of the time.

The French, we know, are noted for being more or less omniscient and versatile men of letters. They in the nineteenth century
with their idealistic bent and their enterprising scholarly spirit
reached out, appropriated, and re-edited the ethics and philosophy,

[1] Q. v. R. W. Emerson, The Superlative, in Literary and Biographical Sketches.

Transcendental in tone, of various other countries. The French Eclectics of the Restoration Period, in other words, were instrumental in making France a kind of meeting ground of German, Scottish, and English idealism, — the idealism of Fichte and Kant, of Reid and Stewart, of Cudworth and Price. And the familiarity of the New-England idealists, as evinced in *The Dial*, the "Specimens of Foreign Standard Literature," and the writings of Ripley, Fuller, Alcott, Emerson, and others, with the writings of the, broadly speaking, omniscient and versatile French Eclectics, materially helped, indeed, to transplant Transcendentalism from Europe in the nineteenth century and to establish it on New-England soil.

The overlapping of literature with philosophy and of philosophy with literature is, moreover, a noteworthy trait in consonance with French genius. Cousin and Jouffroy occupied professorial chairs of literature as well as philosophy. Their philosophical writings have a literary flavor and their words on literature have a philosophical tone. Such, too, is distinctly the case with the writings of George Ripley, Margaret Fuller, A. Bronson Alcott, and Ralph Waldo Emerson. Although these representative New-England Transcendentalists were philosophical in spirit, they, like the French Eclectics who were at once their predecessors and contemporaries, are quite literary in style of expression and in many of their personal tastes. And the analogy between the French Eclectics and the New-England Transcendentalists, in regard to the dovetailing in their writings of literature and philosophy is, along with other features in common, more or less interesting and significant.

A few observations concerning the mission of Transcendentalism, as manifested in greater or less degree in the writings of the French Eclectics and in the writings of the New-England idealists, may be in order by way of conclusion.

Poets, we are told, are liberating gods,[1] and what is said to be true of poets may be said to be true of Transcendentalists; for

---

[1] *Q. v.* Emerson, Essay, The Poet. Also cf. Cousin, page 35: "The characteristic of inspiration is enthusiasm; it is accompanied with that forcible emotion,

Transcendentalists, as regards point of view, are to be ranged among the poets of the world. They are like the good seed which falls on good ground. They affirm life hopefully and faithfully, and affirm it, too, more abundantly.

The world in which we live here below is, as we all know, strange and precarious. Nature is cold and unfeeling, impartial and inexorable. The sun shines and the rain falls on good and evil alike. Babylon and Ninevah have vanished from the earth like the snows of last winter. Vice and virtue appear to be products of peculiar conditions like vitriol and sugar. The pendulum of humanity's thought is continually swinging between altruism and egoism, idealism and materialism. Who among us stands on firm ground? Upon what can any of us pin our faith? The Transcendentalist would rely upon the life of the Infinite and Eternal flowing through him more or less fully and freely, and upon the light of the Infinite and Eternal shining in him in the course of time more and more purely and brightly. We are not, according to his principles, finite creatures below on earth with an autocratic Jehovah in the heavens above, but are all a part of a divine Cosmic Whole. In the midst of which, in one form after another, through myriads of millenniums, and countless adverse experiences, human consciousness has been developing. The same wonderful impulses and instincts which guide the ant and the bee and the bird in their ways also constitute in us, on a higher plan, divine immanence, and move us from age to age to greater wisdom and power, and deepen in us insight into truth and beauty.[1]

" The materialist," Emerson writes, " insists on facts, on history, on the force of circumstances, and the animal wants of man; the idealist, on the power of thought and of will, on inspiration, on miracle, on individual culture. The idealist concedes all that the other affirms, and then asks for his grounds of assurance that things are as his senses represent them." And again Emerson

which bears the soul away from its ordinary and subaltern state and disengages from it the sublime and godlike portion of its nature. The language of inspiration is poetry."

[1] Cf. Jouffroy, Facts of Man's Moral Nature: "Toward this good (the satisfaction of our entire nature) all passions of every kind aspire; and it is this good (God) which our nature is impelled with every unfolding faculty to seek." Q. v. page 44.

writes, giving us the key of the mission of Transcendentalism: "The positivists' appeal to the idealist to leave his idealism to strengthen the ranks of reform and regenerate society is irony's *ne plus ultra.* Its answer is Moses and the prophets; its answer is Christ and the Church; its answer is Luther and Calvin and John Knox; its answer is Cromwell and Milton and Vane, Plymouth Rock and Bunker Hill; its answer is Rousseau and Turgot, the voice of Fichte amidst Napoleon's drums, Cobden and the Corn-law Rhymes, Mazzini and Gladstone; its answer is Garrison, the Emancipation Proclamation, and the Scaffold of John Brown; its answer is the Transcendental movement in New England." [1]

[1] Cf. Cousin, Introduction à l'histoire de la philosophie, 10 leçon, 1828: "Ce qui est vrai d'un peuple est vrai de tous les autres d'une époque et de toutes les époques; donc l'histoire entière est représentée par les grands hommes. Donnez-moi la série des grands hommes, tous les grands hommes connus, et je vous ferai l'histoire du genre humain."

BIBLIOGRAPHY

ALCOTT, AMOS BRONSON.
  Concord Days, 1872.
  Conversations with Children on the Gospels, 1836.
  Emerson, 1865.
  New Connecticut (Poem), 1881.
  Observations on the Principles and Methods of Infant Instruction, 1830.
  Diary, March, 1835.
  Pythagorean Sayings, *The Dial*, April, 1842.
  Orphic Sayings, *The Dial*, April, 1843.
  Spiritual Culture, Boston, 1841.
ALCOTT, LOUISA MAY.
  Life, Letters, and Journals.   Edited by Ednah D. Cheney, Boston, 1889.
AUSTIN, SARAH.
  The S ate of Public Ins'ruction in Prussia. Trans. from Cousin, N. Y., 1389.

BAKEWELL, CHARLES M.
  Source Book in Ancient Philosophy, N. Y., 1907.
BALDWIN, JAMES MARK.
  Dictionary of Philosophy and Psychology, N. Y. and London, 1901–1905.
BARRETT, B. F.
  Swedenborg and Channing, Boston, 1878.
BELLEISLE, RENÉ DE POYEN.
  A French View of Emerson, Boston, 1885.
BIBLIOTHECA INDIA.
  Calcutta, 1852.
BONALD, LOUIS GABRIEL AMBROSE.
  Observations sur l'ouvrage de Mme. de Staël, Paris, 1818.
BOOTH, MARY L.
  Secret History of the French Court under Richelieu and Maza in, N. Y., 1859.

CABOT, JAMES ELLIOTT.
  Memoir of Ralph Waldo Emerson, 2 vols., Cambridge, 1887.
CARO, ELME MARIE.
  Philosophie et philosophes, Paris, 1888.
CAROVÉ, F. W.
  Religion und Philosophie in Frankreich, Göttingen, 1827.
CHANNING, WILLIAM ELLERY.
  Sermons, *q. v.* Works, First Complete Am. Ed., Boston, 1841.
CHANNING, WILLIAM HENRY.
  Critical Survey of Moral Systems.   Trans. from Cousin, Boston, 1840.
  Introduction to Ethics.   Trans. from Cousin, Boston, 1845.
  The Life of W. E. Channing, Boston, 1880.

CLARKE, JAMES FREEMAN.
Memoir of Ralph Waldo Emerson, Boston, 1885.
COOKE, GEORGE WILLIS.
The Dial. See Journal of Speculative Philosophy, July, 1885.
Ralph Waldo Emerson, Boston, 1882.
The Poets of Transcendentalism, Boston and N. Y., 1903.
COUSIN, VICTOR.
Fragments philosophiques, 1826–1828.
Cours d'histoire de la philosophie, 1827–1840.
Cours d'histoire de la philosophie morale, au XVIII siècle, 1840–1841.
Des pensées de Pascal, 1842.
Du vrai, du beau, et du bien, 1854.
Histoire générale de la philosophie, 1864.
    Translations:
Preface to Tenneman's Manual. Trans. by G. Ripley, Boston, 1838.
Preface to Philosophical Fragments. Trans. by G. Ripley, Boston, 1838.
Preface to New Philosophical Fragments. Trans. by G. Ripley, Boston, 1838.
History of Moral Philosophy of the Eighteenth Century. Trans. by C. S. Henry, N. Y., 1838.
Introduction to the History of Philosophy. Trans. by H. G. Linberg, Boston, 1832.
The Philosophy of the Beautiful. Trans. by J. C. Daniel, N. Y., 1849.

DAMISON, PH.
Essais sur l'histoire de la philosophie en France au XIX siècle, Paris, 1828.
DANIEL, J. C.
The Philosophy of the Beautiful. Trans. from Cousin, N. Y., 1849.
DESCARTES, RENÉ.
Discours de la méthode, Paris, 1637.
DEWEY, JOHN.
Exposition of Kant's Philosophy, q. v. Dict. of Phil. and Psy.
DIAL, THE, Boston, 1840–1844.

EMERSON, MARY MOODY,
q. v. Literary and Biographical Studies by R. W. Emerson.
EMERSON, RALPH WALDO.
Complete Works, with a biographical introduction and notes. Century ed., 12 vols., Boston, 1903–1904.
ETHNICAL SCRIPTURES,
q. v. The Dial, July, 1843.

FAGUET, ÉMILE.
Politiques et moralistes du dix-neuvième siècle, Paris, 1898.
FOURIER, FRANÇOIS CHARLES MARIE.
Théorie des Quatre Mouvements, Lyon, 1808.
Traité d'association domestique agricole, Paris, 1822.
Le nouveau monde industriel, Besançon, 1829.
La fausse industrie morcelées, Paris, 1835.
FOURIERISM.
By E. P. P. The Dial, April, 1844.
FROMMAN'S Klassiker der Philosophie.
Immanuel Kant, sein Leben und seine Lehre, Stuttgart, 1898.
FROTHINGHAM, OCTAVIUS BROOKS.
Transcendentalism in New England, Boston, 1903.

FRUITLANDS.
The Dial, July, 1843.
FULLER, SARAH MARGARET.
The Dial, 1840–1844.
At Home and Abroad, Boston, 1856.
Life Without and Life Within, Boston, 1859.
Woman in the Nineteenth Century, N. Y., 1845.
Papers on Literature and Art, N. Y., 1846.

HAWTHORNE, NATHANIEL.
The Blithedale Romance.
HEDGE, F. H.
History as a Manifestation of Spirit (from Hegel).
Atheism in Philosophy, Boston, 1884.
German Prepositions, Cambridge, 1875.
The Nineteenth Century, Christ. Exam., May, 1850.
HENRY CALEB SPRAGUE.
Elements of Psychology, N. Y., 1838. Trans. from Cousin.
History of Moral Philosophy of the Eighteenth Century, N. Y., 1838. Trans.
    from Cousin.

JANET, PAUL.
Le spiritualisme français au XIX siècle, q. v. Revue des Deux Mondes,
    vol. 75, 1868.
Victor Cousin, q. v. Revue des Deux Mondes, fer. 1867.
JOHNSON, SAMUEL.
Transcendentalism, q. v. Radical Review, Boston, Jan., 1884.
JONES, SIR WM.
Laws of Menu, q. v. The Dial, July, 1843.
JOUFFROY, THÉODORE.
Mélanges philosophiques, 1833.
Nouveaux Mélanges, 1842.
Cours de droit naturel, 3 vols., 1835–1842.
Cours d'esthétique, 1843.
    Translations:
Critical Survey of Moral Systems. Trans. by W. H. Channing, Boston 1840.
Introduction to Ethics. Trans. by W. H. Channing, Boston, 1845.
Problem of Human Destiny. Trans. by R. N. Toppan, N. Y., 1862.
Moral Facts of Human Nature. Trans. by R. N. Toppan, N. Y., 1862.
Theoretical Views. Trans. by R. N. Toppan, N. Y., 1862.
JOURNAL OF SPECULATIVE PHILOSOPHY.
Article in The Dial, July, 1885.
JULLEVILLE, PETIE DE.
Histoire de la Langue et de la Littérature française, Paris, 1899.

KANT, IMMANUEL.
By Fredrich Paulsen, Stuttgurt, 1898.

LANSON, GUSTAVE.
Histoire de la littérature française, Paris, 1898.
LAUN, HENRI VAN.
History of French Literature, 1892.
LINBERG, H. G.
Introduction to the History of Philosophy. Trans. from Cousin, Boston,
    1832.

MATHLAE, A.
Manuale di Filosafia, Lugano, 1829.
MIGNET, FRANÇOIS AUGUST.
Éloges Historiques, Paris, 1880.

NETTEMENT, ALFRED.
Histoire de la Littérature française sous la Restauration, Paris, 1853.
NEW CENTURY DICTIONARY AND CYCLOPEDIA.
The Century Company, N. Y., 1897.

OLLE-LAPRUNE, LÉON.
Théodore Jouffroy, Paris, 1899.
OSSOLI.
See Fuller, Sarah Margaret.

PARKER, THEODORE.
Complete Works, London, 1876.
German Literature, q. v. The Dial, January, 1841.
PAULSEN, FRIEDRICH.
Immanuel Kant, Stuttgart, 1898.
PEABODY, ELIZABETH PALMER.
Record of a School, Boston, 1835.
Reminiscences of Rev. W. E. Channing, Boston, 1880.
PHILO.
An Evangeliad, by Sylvester Judd, Boston, 1850.

RAVAISSON, FELIX.
La Philosophie en France au XIX siècle, Paris, 1857.
RÉMUSAT, CHARLES DE.
Critiques et Études Littéraires, Paris, 1880.
RENAN, ERNEST.
Essais de Morale et de critique, Paris, 1860.
REVUE DES DEUX MONDES.
Le Spiritualisme français au XIX siècle, vol. 75, 1868.
RIPLEY, GEORGE.
Specimens of Foreign Standard Literature, 14 vols. Hilliard, Gray, & Co.,
Boston, 1838.
Translations of:
Preface to Tenneman's Manual (C.).
Preface to Philosophical Fragments (C.).
Preface to New Philosophical Fragments (C.).
Preface to Translation of Dugald-Stewart (J.).
Philosophical Miscellanies (J.).
ROGERS, ARTHUR KENYON.
A Student's History of Philosophy, N. Y., 1902.
ROYCE, JOSIAH.
The Spirit of Modern Philosophy, Boston, 1892.

SAINT-HILAIRE, BARTHÉLEMY.
Victor Cousin, Paris, 1895.
SANBORN, FRANK.
Ralph Waldo Emerson, Boston, 1901.
SIMON, JULES.
Victor Cousin, Paris, 1887.
STAËL, MADAME LA BARONNE.
Œuvres complètes, Paris, 1810, 1816.

TAINE, ADOLPHE HIPPOLYTE.
Les origines de la France contemporaine, N. Y., 1895.
THOREAU, HENRY DAVID.
Walden, Cambridge, 1887.
TOPPAN, ROBERT N.
Problem of Human Destiny (J), N. Y., 1862.
Moral Facts of Human Nature (J), N. Y., 1862.
Theoretical Views (J), N. Y., 1862.
TRANSCENDENTALISM DEFINED,
q. v. The Dial, July, 1841.

UEBERWEG, FRIEDRICH.
History of Philosophy. Trans., N. Y., 1898.
UNITARIAN MOVEMENT IN NEW ENGLAND.
The Dial, April, 1841.

VACHEROT, ÉTIENNE.
La situation philosophique en France, q. v. Revue de Deux Mondes, vol. 75, 1868.
VATTIER, GUSTAVE.
Galerie des académiciens, Paris, 1863–1866.

WEBER, EMILE ALFRED.
History of Philosophy. Trans., N. Y., 1896.
WENDELL, BARRETT.
A Literary History of America, N. Y., 1900.
WIGHT, O. W.
History of Modern Philosophy. Trans. from Cousin, N. Y., 1852.
WILKINS, CHARLES.
Veeshnu Sarma, q. v. The Dial, July, 1843.
WYZEWA, TEODORE.
Pages Choisies (de Cousin), Paris, 1898.